CHOOSE SPIRIT NOW

Wake Up to an Exquisite Life

GINGER GRAF DUNAWAY

BALBOA.
PRESS

A DIVISION OF HAY HOUSE

Balboa Press books may be ordered through booksellers or by contacting:

Balboa Press
A Division of Hay House
1663 Liberty Drive
Bloomington, IN 47403
www.balboapress.com
1 (877) 407-4847

Because of the dynamic nature of the Internet, any web addresses or links contained in this book may have changed since publication and may no longer be valid. The views expressed in this work are solely those of the author and do not necessarily reflect the views of the publisher, and the publisher hereby disclaims any responsibility for them.

The author of this book does not dispense medical advice or prescribe the use of any technique as a form of treatment for physical, emotional, or medical problems without the advice of a physician, either directly or indirectly. The intent of the author is only to offer information of a general nature to help you in your quest for emotional and spiritual well-being. In the event you use any of the information in this book for yourself, which is your constitutional right, the author and the publisher assume no responsibility for your actions.

Any people depicted in stock imagery provided by Thinkstock are models, and such images are being used for illustrative purposes only.
Certain stock imagery © Thinkstock.

Printed in the United States of America.

ISBN: 978-1-4525-9827-7 (sc)
ISBN: 978-1-4525-9829-1 (hc)
ISBN: 978-1-4525-9828-4 (e)

Library of Congress Control Number: 2014919877

Balboa Press rev. date: 01/21/2015

This book is dedicated to my parents and family. Thank you, Mom and Dad, for being such wonderful parents and for each of you teaching me in your own special way to look to the Holy Spirit within, our higher self, for guidance and strength. And to my own family, my absolutely amazing husband, Mark, and our heart and soul and breath, Rowen. And to all of you out there, believe it or not, you were a part of this book coming together. A part of you was ready, a part of you wanted to hear what is in these pages … and so this book came to be.

Thank you, Dad, for always reminding me to see the miracle in all things, in every situation. Without you, in more ways than one, I wouldn't be where I am. And I am truly grateful for this eternal moment in which I have found myself, most of the time, in which I feel it: the Oneness, the light, the joy, the love. Namaste.

Cover design inspired by my talented friend and graphic artist Nadine Dalati.

Choose Spirit Now logo designed partially by Ginger and Rowen Dunaway and put into full creative reality by Nadine Dalati.

Thank you, Nadine, for being able to create something so amazing from a vague description of what I envision.

Author photograph taken by our talented local photographer, Laura Cantrell of Laura Cantrell Photography.

For information on Kripalu yoga, visit *www.kripalu.org,* and for more information on *A Course in Miracles,* visit *www.facim.org.*

CONTENTS

Part III
Beyond the Ego Cloud

INTRODUCTION

My Dad always told me that as a baby I smiled a lot. He said he always wondered who and what I would become because of that. It took a childhood hardship to cause me to lose that smile for a long while.

In my late teens and early twenties I had perfect strangers on a regular basis tell me to smile because God loved me. I once had a monk at a temple on Kauai whom I had just met, ask me in his Indian accent *"Why so serious, Ginger?"* as he pointed to the semi-permanent furrow between my brow. I had been in what seemed constant thought and analysis ever since my childhood hardship, searching far and wide to find that smile again within myself.

When I first heard about being content in the present moment, I got the concept but had no idea that it was really possible. How do I even begin to get to the now? How can I silence all the crap that keeps me from it? And once I found the now, would I really be able to enjoy it?

I'll never forget hearing things like *a new car won't make you happy.* "What?"
A perfect relationship won't make you happy. "Are you serious?"
A million dollars won't make you happy. "Are you sure?"

These external objects of desire brought on a momentary feeling of happiness (I never had a million dollars), but I soon felt let down when I realized they couldn't *keep* me feeling this way. Finding happiness and contentment from within in the present moment sounded great, but where in the world did I even start? Was this the key in bringing my smile back?

Once I began my hatha yoga practice (also considered movement meditation), I finally caught glimpses of what it meant to be in the now and be totally content. Through the practice I began to release old anger and baggage from childhood and experience a peace and contentment that I hadn't felt much in my adult life. I felt that the yoga practice was doing a world of good, but I also felt that there was something holding me back that I couldn't put my finger on. That's where *A Course in Miracles* (ACIM) came in.

ACIM introduced me to the ego in a depth that I had not previously known. Even my studies in Psychology, Human Development and various self-help and spiritual books didn't come close to preparing me for what ACIM brought to the table. After reading ACIM I went back and re-read the *Yoga Sutras*, statements on yoga written about two thousand years ago. I was astounded at how similar these teachings were and spent the next several years being guided to write *Choose Spirit Now*.

What I have found is that a blend of both yoga and ACIM helps us immensely in our vigilance over the ego playing out in our lives so that we can *choose* to awaken from it. Yes, it is our choice to awaken from the ego and once you learn yogic and Course concepts you will feel a world of relief as it sinks in that this choice really is yours. A combination of this ancient practice and philosophy of yoga and the principles and practice of *A Course in Miracles* has led me to live a mostly peaceful life. I am not perfect, but I now know that this imperfection is the ego, and I forgive myself for it every day. I finally found my smile again. It's not planted on my face all the time, but it rests ever present within, leading me to live a truly exquisite life, and for that I am truly grateful.

For all the yogis out there, if you suspect the ego is hiding out in your practice, this is your ticket to clear it out. For all the Course students out there, if you find yourself wanting a ritual or practice that naturally brings you into deep self-study and connection with the Holy Spirit, then this will show you how. You will be amazed at how similar yoga is to Course teachings and how the practice can deepen your studies. For anyone else wanting to live an exquisite life, read on.

If you love this book and would like to experience it as an online retreat, visit *www.choosespiritnow.com*.

Namaste means "the light in me is the light in you." In other words, we are One and the same.

Namaste, my friend.

PART I

Understanding the Ego Cloud

CHAPTER 1

The Childhood Drama

The happy childhood is hardly worth your while.
—Frank McCourt *Angela's Ashes:*
A Memoir (McCourt 1999, 11)

My Initial Introduction to Ego

I am grateful that my childhood was far from perfect. It led me to where I am now; it began my path toward awakening.

My dad flirted with another woman. It was the first crack in my perception of the world and the biggest life-changing event I ever went through. Like a lot of women do when this happens, my mom made him "pay" with reenacted nightly dramas, fueled by a jealousy-induced temporary lack of sanity. They fought almost every night until the wee hours of the morning for almost three years.

While watching my dad *pay* for his mistakes, my siblings and I got our first lesson in having the rug pulled out from underneath us. I was the youngest of three, and eight years old at the time. I can still remember the absolute anguish and agony my mother was in at the deep, potent feeling of betrayal. At the time, all I wanted was to see my mom happy again. But, as most of us understand, once someone feels betrayed in a relationship, it is very difficult to get that trust and security back. The ego wreaks havoc on the mind and the emotions, as events are replayed over and over in the mind's eye like a mental torture chamber.

I have a brother six years older and a sister four years older, and we three took on various roles to keep our family together. My brother, Curtis, played the peacekeeper. He was always trying to keep the peace between my parents, but he also kept my sister and me feeling safe as best he could, always explaining to us what things meant and giving us his prediction of things to come. My sister, Suzette, was the rebel, always calling my parents out on how they were handling the situation and pleading with them to stop. My brother and sister became lifelines for me in a rough and rocky sea.

I remember the three of us holed up in my brother's room, discussing the fighting going on in the room next to us and feeling safe in each other's company. At least I wasn't alone. I was the observer, taking it all in and learning to absorb and adapt in this new, high-stress environment. We stayed up with our parents every night and tried to keep them—and my whole world—from breaking up and falling apart.

I'll never forget, at eight years old, walking down the covered, open-air hallway at Julius T. Wright Preparatory School for Girls, with rain coming down all around me and thinking, *Oh my God, is this really happening to my family?* It felt very surreal. At the end of that year, I received a perfect-attendance award at our school's awards ceremony, and I remember my mom crying afterward in disbelief that I had made it to school every day that year, after staying up most nights until two or three in the morning.

The truth is, I felt like I was having the life sucked out of me. My safe, secure environment had crumbled in front of my eyes, and for the first time, my world began turning gray.

As a young girl, I didn't understand what was happening to my mom. All I knew was that I loved her, and I just wanted things to be normal again. It was difficult seeing my dad cry and plead with her to stop the ranting. It was difficult seeing them both in so much pain. Over the next several years, the fighting lessened, and once my brother went off to college, it stopped. As I reached my late teens and early twenties, I began blaming Mom for what she had put us through. I wish I could say that I blamed my dad equally for not being able to stop it and for his flirtation to begin with, but since Mom had the more dominant, fiery personality it was easier to outwardly blame her more.

It wasn't until much later that I realized Mom was simply experiencing the beast of the ego, something we all struggle with on a daily basis. I was witnessing in these nightly dramas all the deeply held fears and insecurities that plagued my mom, as they had plagued her mom, which would later plague me in my own life. My mom had watched her own mother go through betrayal. When she saw Dad flirting with another woman, it triggered the memories of what her mother went through, and she reacted the best way she knew how, as she had learned from her own mother.

I know how much my mom loves us, and I know that she would have stopped this nightly drama if she could have. The problem was, she couldn't stop it. The feelings of anger and betrayal were too strong. My mom's need for answers that would never come, for justice that would never be enough, for do-overs that were impossible to come by, drove her rants, filled with anger and anguish.

As the nightly dramas unfolded, my siblings and I soaked up this deep fear and insecurity; and this vicious cycle of *vasana* and *samskara* (Sanskrit terms we will get to later) was to now play out over three generations. I did not realize it at the time, but this started a fire in me, a fire that would drive me to understand what was happening and figure out how the hell to stop it.

Super-Tuned Radar

There is a quote from Frank McCourt's *Angela's Ashes: A Memoir* that says, "the happy childhood is hardly worth your while" (1999, 11). I read this book when I was in my early twenties, and it made me realize that I was grateful for the fighting and drama that was acted out in front of me night after night. I felt it made me more sensitive and empathetic to others pain and insecurity.

Somehow, among the drama going on within our house, we had still managed to have a lot of great times. As a matter of fact, most of our friends thought, from the outside looking in, that we had the perfect family. But by my twenties, I felt like a desert wasteland inside, dying to be soothed, comforted, and loved. I suffered through unspeakable anger and emotional pain, but I used this raw emotion to become hypersensitive, hyper-aware of others' emotional states, especially in regard to relationships.

I turned into a super-tuned radar in social situations, to men who were flirting with other women who were not their significant other. I had such painful emotional empathy for these women, many of whom I didn't even know. I tormented myself, watching the fidgeting, nervous laughter, and burning looks in these women's eyes, trying to telepathically urge their men to stop gawking at another woman. It burned me up inside. I found myself totally distrustful of men, crazy jealous of other women, and needing drama in my own relationship for it to feel meaningful at all.

Becoming this super-tuned radar perfectly prepared me for the search I was then to go on, to try to find that trust and security again in my own life. I sought a way out of on-again-off-again depression, fueled by my feelings of fear, jealousy, and insecurity. I would eventually find a spiritual teaching that would lead me much further than simply finding self-esteem or a way out of depression. I would find what it means to be awake, enlightened—a concept that I had heard of but never knew was possible to understand fully.

Yogis Call it *Samvega*. What in the World Is *Samvega?*

Patanjali is believed to be the person who wrote the *Yoga Sutras* two thousand years ago. The *Yoga Sutras* are threads or statements on yoga. There are four short chapters to the sutras, each with short statements shedding light on what this ancient practice does for us. Stephen Cope talks about the sutras in his book, *The Wisdom of Yoga*. He says, "Patanjali introduces the term *samvega* in the first chapter of the *Yoga Sutra*—using the word to indicate a 'wholehearted' (or 'vehement') determination to find a way out of suffering" (Cope 2006, 15). Cope goes on to say that *samvega* is "a complex state involving a kind of disillusionment with mundane life, and a wholehearted longing for a deeper investigation into the inner workings of the mind and the self" (Cope 13). *Samvega* is that initial drive we all have inside to understand what the meaning of life is. Why do we experience suffering, and if there is a way out of it within this lifetime, then what in the world is it?

This is what I love about studying yoga. We realize that the yogis thousands of years ago were searching for the same things we are searching for today: happiness that lasts, fulfillment that lasts. This "suffering" Patanjali writes about is something we can all relate to. It could be suffering from past traumatic experiences; it could be the usual stress, fear, worry, and anxiety you feel on a daily basis; it could be the discomforts of jealousy and competition with coworkers, family, or friends; it could be gossip that you find yourself participating in that drains your life force; it could be anger, guilt, and resentment preventing you from forgiving someone, and maybe that someone is yourself. But the bottom line is we are all looking to end our suffering, however that suffering is playing out in our lives, and find that peace within.

Even when life is pretty good, there can still be a sense that something is missing, that we are not completely happy or fulfilled. There may be a sense of guilt for even feeling this way, because from the outside looking in, we *should* be happy. We can have days when life is beautiful and perfect and then the next day find ourselves in the depths of hell, with thoughts of worthlessness and inadequacy. This is what the yogis call *duhka*, dissatisfaction in life, and it leads us to *samvega*, that determination to find a better way.

We have to go beyond trying to alleviate our suffering and look at understanding what's causing our suffering to begin with. We can fix and patch all we want, but until we *understand* the cause, more suffering will just keep arising.

Yoga and *A Course in Miracles*

Yoga and ACIM both recognize the ego as the cause of all suffering and give step-by-step processes to awaken us out of the ego's grip, out of suffering, to the peace, happiness, and fulfillment that is here for us in every moment.

What? Wow!

7

That's what this book is all about: learning the tools and processes from yoga and ACIM to understand what the ego really is, how to awaken out of its thought system, and how to strengthen and deepen trust in our own inner guidance to help us find what we've truly been searching for all along: happiness and fulfillment that lasts; an awakening to the peace within; an awakening to our Oneness with each other and all of creation; but most importantly revealing our constant union and connection with God Himself.

Living awake is the most important thing you can be doing for yourself, your loved ones, and the world around you. Once we uncover this light inside of ourselves, the most amazing thing happens: we bring an unfathomable amount of light into the world. We find ourselves guided to live in the perfect way to benefit ourselves, our loved ones, and the world around us. In other words, we positively affect the world in ways beyond our human mind's comprehension, just by finding that peace within, just by remembering our Oneness with each other. Now you find yourself guided effortlessly from this peaceful, connected state, guided to live in a way that is good for the whole of creation.

This sounds simple enough, but the ego—which we will talk about in much detail throughout this book—is so complex that it can make it very difficult to awaken from. The ego is simply a thought system, a belief system that we all get immersed in as we build this system from the ground up, learning much of it from parents, caregivers, and friends. As a matter of fact, many people are so immersed that they won't ever be able to see their way out in this lifetime. We are our own worst enemy here. We are so immersed in the ego's thought system and belief system that we don't even know how deeply we are affected by it or how much it is literally running the show. And most importantly we certainly don't realize that it blocks us from remembering or experiencing our connection with God.

Think of it this way: before it was proved that the world was round, could you imagine trying to convince someone that they were really living on a huge, round planet spinning around the sun? People would look at you like you were crazy! Well, when we are told that we are living in a mind-set (the ego) that is completely running the show, that is completely responsible for our suffering in many forms, that is actually blocking us from feeling whole and complete as a part of God, we think, *No way; that's impossible!*

Here's the good news: yoga is a practice thousands of years old, which is meant to lead one out of this ego mind-set. We will be learning the ego's mind tricks and temptations, which have been written about in ancient Eastern scriptures called the *Vedas* at least four thousand years ago and again in the *Yoga Sutras* two thousand years ago. How amazing is it that this ego thought system and belief system that is still negatively affecting us today was written about four thousand years ago? How amazing is it that we have a movement-meditation practice (yoga poses) as well as seated-meditation practice, all designed to awaken us from this ego mind-set to what yoga calls our true nature—our true nature that we are tuned in to at birth but quickly forget because of the ego's thought system that quickly gets built up around us, clouding it from sight? How amazing is it that this practice of yoga brings us deep peace and higher guidance as it awakens us from the ego to reveal our constant connection with God Himself? This ancient practice of yoga is absolutely amazing to me, and I believe that this 'waking up' is what life should be all about!

A Course in Miracles (ACIM) is a text written back in the 1970s by a woman named Helen Schucman. It took her about seven years to write it, and she was writing it from what she called the voice of Jesus dictating these teachings to her. ACIM works on the level of the mind, to awaken us again from the ego mind-set. It also contains a workbook with daily reading lessons to reflect upon to help assimilate the teachings of the text into daily life. The Course helps us to shed layer by layer of the ego's thought system and belief system, by strengthening our relationship with the Holy Spirit. The ego can be very tricky, and while we are still immersed in it, we need help from the Holy Spirit to guide us out. (In chapter 6 we will be defining Holy Spirit in a whole new way for us to really understand what it is.) If you can believe that ACIM is Jesus' teachings, then these teachings are actually two thousand years old but brought to light again in this sacred text.

ACIM can be difficult to grasp when you first begin reading it, but little by little, as you begin to shed layer by layer of the ego's thought system, suddenly you find yourself living a whole different life, one filled with love, peace, and joy. You find yourself open to loving and forgiving, as Jesus did. If you try to read the Course and it seems like too much for you, there are all sorts of other books that soften some of the ideas of the Course and may be a better fit for you for now. I started out learning Course concepts from Gary Renard's book, *The Disappearance of the Universe,* a suggestion from my dad. It was still a tough read, but it laid the groundwork for me to be able to read ACIM three years later.

Reading *Disappearance* was a huge reality check. I was told by my mentor in massage school eight years earlier that sometimes brainwashing is a good thing. Her idea stayed with me, and once I read *Disappearance,* it was like an invitation to really scrutinize my belief system and recognize that it was a learned system based off of my parents' and society's deeply held beliefs. In my twenties and early thirties, I had a chance to really see if I believed these in my core or if there were other beliefs that rang true for me that could heal my aching soul. Over the next two to three years, my mind went through such a miraculous rewiring, thanks to Gary's book and the Course's concepts.

It was like I had found a light to guide me out of the darkness the ego had bound me in. I realized that all of those years spent feeling achingly lonely was all due to my seeming separation from God. And all those years, the Holy Spirit had been listening, giving me stepping stone after stepping stone to guide me out of the ego's stronghold. My grandfather always told my mom when she was experiencing a problem, "Steady as you go, Carole; steady as you go." I now felt God and the Holy Spirit (my higher self) steadily working on me, whispering these words to me. "Steady as you go, Ginger, steady as you go," as I stayed the course and began shedding layer by layer of my ego's thought and belief system.

Meditation Journaling Exercise

Before you read any further, I'd like you to answer a couple of questions. I want your answers to arise effortlessly in your mind, so take a moment to get relaxed and soften your gaze. Sit nice and tall, wherever you are.

Lengthen through the crown of the head, relax the shoulders, relax the face, and take a nice deep breath into the lower belly, into the entire torso. Now read over the following questions and simply allow the answers to arise in your mind.

Journaling Questions

- What are you hoping to gain from a book such as this?
- What is going on in your life specifically that you feel you could use some guidance with? (Stress, anxiety, fear, insecurity, jealousy, worry, judgments on yourself and others.)
- Are you simply looking for another book to keep you on your path, to keep you in your awakening, making way for more peace, love, and joy in your daily life?

Whatever the answers, this book will support you.

Keep your answers in a journal. It's always fun to go back and see how far you've come in understanding and rising out of the ego along the way.

In the next chapter we will learn the most important truth that we tend to forget amid this human experience and begin to bring common sense to some spiritual beliefs that most of us already have. This is the equivalent of turning on the flashlight within this ego cloud and begin shining the light on what is really going on here. How exciting!

CHAPTER 2

It's as Simple as This: We've Forgotten Who We Really Are

These bodies come to an end; but that vast embodied Self is ageless, fathomless, eternal.
>—Krishna speaking to Arjuna in the *Bhagavad Gita* translated by Stephen Mitchell (Mitchell 2000, 49)

We Have Forgotten Who We Really Are

All of our problems are due to one thing: we have forgotten who we really are.

What does this mean?

We have literally forgotten that we were created perfectly in God's image. God is love, perfect in peace, love, and joy, and He created us in His image. (We will look at this more closely in chapter 4.) We get that, but then again, we don't really get that.

Did you roll your eyes and look the other way just because I said "God, peace, love, and joy" all in the same sentence? That's part of our problem. Some of us have been so disenfranchised by

Some of us have been so disenfranchised by past meanings and associations from religions or spiritual traditions that we shy away from any talk of God whatsoever. We assume we are being sacrilegious by talking about God in depth outside the norm, or we roll our eyes and think, *Here comes the holy roller crapola*, if God is brought up at all.

past meanings and associations from religions or spiritual traditions that we shy away from any talk of God whatsoever. We assume we are being sacrilegious by talking about God in depth outside the norm, or we roll our eyes and think, *Here comes the holy roller crapola*, if God is brought up at all. We all have different perceptions of God or the Divine, and that's okay. Simply allow yourself to be open for now. This is actually the first step to even begin the process of awakening.

A Course in Miracles and the *Yoga Sutras* both teach that our problems as human beings happen because we have forgotten who we really are and we are misidentifying ourselves with the ego. What in the world is the ego? Let's find out.

The Importance of Looking at Our Beliefs

Let's start understanding the ego and where it comes from, by beginning to take a look at our beliefs.

Most of us have been taught not to question our beliefs and simply to have faith. This is wonderful if you want to stay in suffering. The truth is we aren't trying to change our beliefs but bring common sense to them. Once you do, you will understand how we've tricked ourselves into more suffering.

> Even though we believe we have a soul or spirit that is eternal, within the busyness of our lives, we forget it quite readily and get suckered into the belief that we are humans in bodies that will die one day.

What Are Our Basic Beliefs, and Where Did They Go Awry?

Most people would agree that we are more than these bodies, that we have some sort of soul or spirit that enters the body at birth or conception and then lives on after the body is dead. Even though we believe we have a soul or spirit that is eternal, within the busyness of our lives, we forget it quite readily and get suckered into the belief that we are

> We get so involved in the world and stuck in the fear and the stress that we don't notice we've forgotten the most important truth of all: our truest nature is this Spirit that is eternal and can never be harmed by anything of this world.

humans in bodies that will die one day. This causes all kinds of fear and stress, but we are not aware enough to be able to pinpoint it to this forgetfulness of belief. We get so involved in the world and stuck in the fear and the stress that we don't notice we've forgotten the most important truth of all: our truest nature is this Spirit that is eternal, created by God in His image, and can never be harmed by anything of this world.

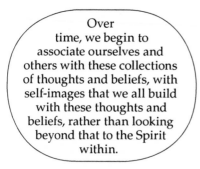

As we move through life, we begin to identify our notion of self solely with the human experience of the body, rather than our eternal nature in Spirit. We are then limiting our identity to the impermanence of the body.

The ego is the sense of self that we all build over time. As we move through life, we begin to identify our notion of self solely with the human experience of the body, rather than our eternal nature in Spirit. We are then limiting our identity to the impermanence of the body. If looked at closely this ego-self is simply a collection of thoughts and beliefs that we all grow into. We each have our own set of thoughts and beliefs: thoughts and beliefs about others, about ourselves, and about the world in general. Some are passed down and learned from caregivers and friends, while others are built from our own past experiences.

As children, we begin to build an ego self-image. This self-image is based on this identification with the body and the circumstances into which we were born, such as who we are, what our beliefs are, and what we are going to do in this life to keep up this self-image. Over time, we begin to associate ourselves and others with these collections of thoughts and beliefs, with self-images that we all build with these thoughts and beliefs, rather than looking beyond that to the Spirit within.

Over time, we begin to associate ourselves and others with these collections of thoughts and beliefs, with self-images that we all build with these thoughts and beliefs, rather than looking beyond that to the Spirit within.

At some point, most of us look up in life and wonder what the hell happened to us. We make the mistake here of simply attributing this life crisis—whenever it happens and no matter how many times it happens—to our childhood loss of innocence. But what we truly lost is the memory of who we really are and where we really came from as perfect creations of God. Now we are mistaking our true nature in Spirit with this ego-self that we have built, and we wonder why we are so unhappy.

We have forgotten that in our truest nature we are pure awareness, or Spirit, in which we are whole, perfect, and eternal: whole as perfect Oneness with all things; perfect as all-loving, all-peaceful, and all-joyful; and eternal with no end. (We will go into more detail about how our true nature is whole, perfect and eternal in chapter 4.) At some point, we developed and began experiencing consciousness within this pure awareness. This consciousness is what allows us to have this amazing human experience, however, this consciousness also allows us to create this ego-self which can begin limiting our consciousness and subsequently limiting our human experience.

The third yoga sutra says, "When the mind has settled, we are established in our essential nature, which is unbounded consciousness." (Shearer, 1982, 90) We experience unbounded consciousness as young children before the ego-self is fully constructed. We can also experience it again in adulthood in rare moments when the mind naturally settles, or through the practice of settling the mind through yoga. In unbounded consciousness we experience what yoga calls *illumined mind* in which the misidentification with ego-self is lifted and there is a sublime awareness of our true nature. However, as long as we allow this ego-self to grow stronger and more distinct, we continue to limit our consciousness to this ego-self with all of its habits and patterns, and then totally misidentify ourselves with this limited ego-consciousness. The fourth yoga sutra says, "Otherwise awareness takes itself to be the patterns of consciousness." (2003, 283) Here the sutras are referring to our ability to misidentify our Self with the ego or ego-consciousness as long as our mind is *not* settled through the practice of yoga.

Consciousness allows us to create this ego-self, but we are not consciously aware of what is happening. All we know is that by the time we reach our teenage years most of us are experiencing suffering on many different levels. We are unaware that what is really happening is our experience of unbounded consciousness is now being limited more and more by all the thoughts, beliefs and judgments that are now running rampant in our heads due to the development of this ego-self. As our consciousness becomes more and more limited and engrossed in the goings on of the ego-self (again, the thoughts, beliefs, and judgments running rampant in our heads) we now *easily* mistake our *selves* for this limited ego-consciousness. We no longer have access to unbounded consciousness and so the awareness of our true nature as whole, perfect, and eternal is long forgotten.

Once we feel cut off from our true nature, we begin searching for wholeness, happiness and perfection again. The problem is, we begin looking for something outside of ourselves to make us *feel* whole, perfect, and happy. We have forgotten that we *already are* whole, perfect, and eternal within our true nature as Spirit, as pure awareness. Once this ego-self is established and consciousness becomes bound by the ego, there is an aspect of our Spirit (Holy Spirit) that calls to us to remember our true nature and wake up from this newfound suffering by guiding us through intuition. The more we identify ourselves with the ego-self, the more difficult it is to notice this higher guidance or trust in it. Now, instead of listening to our intuition, we rely solely on our newfound thought and belief system as we think and analyze our way through life. This only immerses us more deeply into the ego and its thought system as this ego mental construct becomes more and more real to us.

The cycle is endlessly perpetuated, and our relationship with Holy Spirit and God *seemingly* grows more distant. We will be looking at Holy Spirit as our higher self, as a part of our own Spirit that guides us to awaken, which I will explain in more detail in a later chapter. God can be He/She/the Divine/Cosmic Consciousness—whatever your interpretation of God is. Without this strong relationship with our higher self and God, we end up feeling lost. We have forgotten that we are this eternal Spirit: whole, perfect, and immortal. Anytime we feel suffering and pain, we are literally starving for this lost spiritual connection, the only thing that can truly make us feel whole

Anytime we feel suffering and pain, we are literally starving for this lost spiritual connection, the only thing that can truly make us feel whole again, as it reminds us of our union and Oneness with all beings, with all of creation, and most importantly, with God Himself.

16

again, as it reminds us of our union and Oneness with all beings, with all of creation, and most importantly, with God Himself.

In the next chapter we will discuss the search most of us find ourselves on at some point in life and how the ego is responsible for it.

CHAPTER 3

The Search for Home & Ego 101

After long searches here and there, in temples and in
churches, in earths and in heavens, at last you come back,
completing the circle from where you started, to your own
soul …

—Swami Vivekenanda (Cope 1999, 290)

Depression

Since the childhood drama, I was prone to depression; this was my
suffering to bear. I felt very alone and sad and couldn't figure out why.
Little did I know that I was probably experiencing PTSD from living
in such a toxic emotional environment for so long. By this time, my
parents' fighting had stopped for the most part, but my brother, whom
I loved dearly, had gone off to college. I wrote a poem at age eighteen,
explaining this feeling inside of me, titled, "Abyss of Loneliness":

> Loneliness creeps into my room like smoke, quietly, but after
> awhile I begin to smell it and breathe it in, and it begins
> to choke me. But unlike smoke it won't kill me, it will just
> slowly cause my body to melt into a depressing shape. My
> eyes search desperately for a means of escape, but then I
> realize I don't want to escape. I want to become it, so I open
> the gateways of lonely thoughts and let them flow through
> my brain and around my body like a net, trapping me but
> enabling me to see through to the other side, the side I could
> be on but choose not to. The thoughts and feelings are the
> same ones as all the other days and nights, but they are
> magnified this night, bigger and more distinct. Like sharp,

giant thorns burrowing into every cell of my body, piercing
my nerves and pulling the corners of my mouth down hard
as I sob with no clear vision of the end.

I felt very alone, very cut off from anything good or meaningful. I
loved my family, but I also wanted to end the pain and suffering, the
achingly deep loneliness I felt night after night. Little did I know, I had
been cut off completely from what yoga calls my true nature. The ego
had done what it does best in this human experience: it made me forget
who I really was as one with all of creation and with God Himself. It's
interesting, though, how in this poem, I allude to my understanding
that I have a choice to stay in this suffering or cross to the other side.
It's just like the ego and its thought system, to convince us to stay in the
suffering, to wallow in it. It is evident here that I am deeply homesick.
I am lonely for something that I cannot put my finger on, but also, on
some level, I am choosing this suffering.

The Search for Home

I'm about to share two quotes. The first is from an Eastern man, Swami
Vivekenanda, and the second one is from ACIM, so you can imagine
that it's Jesus speaking through this sacred text.
Both of these quotes are beautiful and seem to speak to my soul.

Swami Vivekenanda said:

> After long searches here and there, in temples and in churches,
> in earths and in heavens, at last you come back, completing
> the circle from where you started, to your own soul and find
> that He, for whom you have been seeking all over the world,
> for whom you have been weeping and praying in churches
> and temples, on whom you were looking as the mystery of
> mysteries shrouded in the clouds, is nearest of the near, is your
> own Self, the reality of your life, body and soul. (Cope 1999, 290)

This quote gives us the sense that we are searching for God outside
of ourselves. We have been convinced by our ego-self that we could
never be good enough to find God within us, but once we remember
that God created us *in his image*, then we realize that *in our true nature
as God created us* we must be able to find God's perfection within, God's

wholeness within, and God's eternal nature within. If we go within, we *can* find (remember) what we've truly been searching for: our truest nature as God created us as whole, perfect, and eternal. The problem is when we are immersed in the ego thought system, the ego will convince us that this belief is egotistical (yes, the ego is manipulative enough to use itself to draw us back into its trap) and sacrilegious, thus continuing to fuel our search outside of ourselves. And the cycle continues. The next quote is from ACIM:

> You will undertake a journey because you are not at home in this world. And you will search for your home whether you realize where it is or not. If you believe it is outside you the search will be futile, for you will be seeking it where it is not. You do not remember how to look within for you do not believe your home is there. Yet the Holy Spirit remembers it for you, and He will guide you to your home because that is His mission. As He fulfills His mission He will teach you yours, for your mission is the same as His. (ACIM T-12.IV.5:1-6)

Both these quotes are touching on the fact that we are homesick and we are searching far and wide for *something*, something that fills us up and makes us feel complete. We are searching for our true home. We are searching for God. We are searching for the remembrance of our true nature as whole, perfect, and eternal.

Everything we get or think we want in life is just a poor substitute for what we already *are* in abundance in our true nature, which is our true home. We have this deep memory of our true home and glimpses of it throughout life, but we don't remember how to awaken to it or how to consciously remember it at all. For most of us, our human experience is built upon building the ego which blocks us even more from remembering our true home. It is within us, but we cannot comprehend what this means without first understanding the ego's thought system and how to begin to undo it layer by layer.

The Ego: Constantly Building You Up or Tearing You Down

I grew up with a sister who was always told how beautiful she was; this was hard on me. I never felt pretty. I felt like I was letting my family down for my redheaded, freckle-faced looks. I actually remember my thirteenth birthday, when I opened a gift that was an ugly purse. As I opened it, this thought ran through my head: *An ugly purse for an ugly girl.* But I never wanted to let my mom know how I was feeling, because I felt I would just let her down.

Sometimes at night, I would sob and grab fistfuls of my belly and dig my nails into the skin as I told myself I wasn't good enough or thin enough or pretty enough. I was experiencing the aspect of ego that likes to bash and put down and make me think I'm worthless. On the flip side, I experienced another aspect of ego that told me that one day, I would be good enough. One day, I would get the chance to make these kids see me, really see me, instead of walking right past because I wasn't cute enough to be noticed. I realized much later that this two-faced personality/thought system going on was indicative of the ego and its goal of either tearing me down or falsely building me up. The ego's belief system had been built so strong in me that it had totally cut me off from who I really was inside. Now I was identifying with a negative self-image, and the ego was driving me to be something more.

Ego 101: Where Does Ego Begin?

As babies, we are aware of our underlying connection with everything around us. We are not experiencing the world but are a part of the experience of the world. There is a subtle difference, because before we have a sense of self, we have no way to be an experiencer. We have to develop that sense of self to have something with which to experience the world. Our parents or caregivers are key in this development as we shift from awareness to unbounded consciousness to limited ego-consciousness.

In chapter 4 of the *Yoga Sutras*, sutra 4 says, "Feeling like a self is the frame that orients consciousness toward individuation." (Hartranft 2006, 291) Our parents give us names and begin to *see* us as individuals, which develops that sense of self, that sense of separateness. Mommy and Daddy begin labeling the world around us, further distinguishing our boundaries between "self" and "everything else." I learn that I'm in this body, and I'm called Ginger, and this is my nose, and that's your nose. Once we establish the self, we begin building our self-images, which again are all part of the ego, as a collection of thoughts and

21

beliefs about ourselves, based on what others are mirroring back to us. This shift from awareness to consciousness, and the subsequent identification with the ego-self that we are building, is a necessary development in order to have this human experience.

The bad news is, over time, we lose the remembrance of our true nature and with it the awareness of our underlying spiritual connection with everything around us as we overly identify our "self" with the body and self-image and begin to separate ourselves more and more from our surroundings. We then are subject to experience the separation, imperfection, and fear of mortality that comes with this misidentification with the body and ego-self, leaving us feeling frightened, lost, and incomplete.

The Course says the following:

The body is a tiny fence around a little part of a glorious and complete idea. It draws a circle, infinitely small, around a very little segment of Heaven, splintered from the whole, proclaiming that within it is your kingdom, where God can enter not. (ACIM T-18.VIII.2:5-6)

Within this kingdom the ego rules, and cruelly. And to defend this little speck of dust it bids you fight against the universe. This fragment of your mind is such a tiny part of it that, could you but appreciate the whole, you would see instantly that it is like the smallest sunbeam to the sun, or like the faintest ripple on the surface of the ocean. In its amazing arrogance, this tiny sunbeam has decided it is the sun; this almost imperceptible ripple hails itself as the ocean." (ACIM T-18.VIII.3:1-4)

Ego 101: Ego-Self

Our parents, or caregivers, develop our sense of separation and distinguish our boundaries as an individual being, but depending on what our parents' experiences have been, they also teach us all kinds of things which facilitates the development of our ego-self. We pick up so much from the way our caregivers perceive the world and how they act and react, and we assimilate it into our own experience. We learn their fears, their worries, their behaviors, their thoughts and beliefs (including religious and spiritual beliefs), and their opinions. These religious and spiritual beliefs can be very deeply ingrained. Depending on what they are, some instill love and peace, while others instill fear and guilt. These spiritual and religious belief systems, although they mean well, can end up tempting us to separate ourselves even further from each other because of the different belief structures. From all this learned behavior, belief, etc., we are building a self-image (something we will get into in more detail in a later chapter) and creating deeply ingrained patterns and habits of living.

As we begin to live fully immersed in a mind filled with all these newly learned thoughts, beliefs, etc., our consciousness then mistakes our notion of self with this individual body and all of this noise going on in the mind. This shifts us out of living in the present moment, into living in this made-up mental construct of the ego-self, or ego consciousness. We begin shifting out of being a part of the experience of the world with this underlying sense of connection, into being experiencers of the world and truly feeling separate from it. The more separated and disconnected we feel from others and the world around us, the more apt we are to judge, resist, and analyze our way through life. This only perpetuates the cycle by reinforcing this made-up mental construct. Once the ego-self has been built, it seems to take on a life of its own as it predominantly controls the mind and pretty soon our connection to spirit is long forgotten.

Welcome to the ego.

Ego 101: When the Ego Starts Causing Problems

Once this basic belief of separation has been instilled and we have put deep thought structures into place to support and enhance this belief in separation and the belief in the reality of this made-up mental construct, we totally lose our sense of connection with each other and the world around us. Unless we have a supportive spiritual belief system to remind us of our deeper spiritual connection (Oneness) with all things, we will only be sinking deeper and deeper into this ego-self based on this misidentification with the body and our newfound thought and belief system. This causes all kinds of strife.

If I believe I'm in a body over here and you are in a body over there, then I may fear you can hurt me, or you may fear I can hurt you. I may feel insecure because you could be better than me. When we have this belief that we are separate, then of course we are going to have negative emotions such as fear and insecurity. If we can no longer see our underlying connection with each other and all beings, then we don't seem to care as much how we might be affecting each other and these other beings.

In the second chapter of the *Yoga Sutras,* the third sutra says, "The causes of suffering are not seeing things as they are, the sense of "I," attachment, aversion, and clinging to life" (Hartranft 2003, 285). We will go further into attachment, aversion, and clinging to life as the ego mind tricks later, but this sense of "not seeing things as they really are" really describes our ability to forget where we came from and our ability to forget our sense of connection with all things. This sense of "I" is the notion of self as the body and the self-image that we build over time as we forget where we came from and lose sight of our true nature. The *Yoga Sutras* continue to say in the fourth and fifth sutra, "Not seeing things as they are is the field where the other causes of suffering germinate, whether dormant, activated, intercepted, or weakened. Lacking this wisdom, one mistakes that which is impermanent, impure, distressing, or empty of self for permanence, purity, happiness, and self" (Hartranft 2003, 285). Once we forget where we came from and forget our underlying sense of connection with all things we begin to misidentify ourselves with this ego-self and the impermanent body. This causes suffering, because we can never find permanence, purity, happiness, and self in the ego. We may *think* we have found these qualities of our true nature within the ego at times, but once they fade or disappear, we realize we were mistaken and are usually left feeling devastated.

> We may *think* we have found these qualities of our true nature within the ego at times, but once they fade or disappear, we realize we were mistaken and are usually left feeling devastated.

Ego 101: Where Does the Suffering Come From?

The ego is made up of the learned thoughts, beliefs, and judgments we have about ourselves, the world, and the people around us as we separate ourselves from it and them. The suffering comes from all the negative emotions that stem from these thoughts, beliefs, and judgments we have about ourselves, the world, and others. If I am told constantly as a child that I am worthless, then I come to believe this deeply and can, in turn, feel worthless, sad, and alone. I may end up attacking others, which only ends up proving to me that I am right about myself, making me feel more sad, worthless, and alone.

We begin to allow these thoughts, beliefs, judgments, and the subsequent emotions to drive us in life, rather than allowing Holy Spirit, our higher self, to guide us. Most of us have experiences throughout life in which we know we are being guided by a higher power. But at some point, we become so enmeshed in the ego and its thought and belief system, that we forget how to access this guidance or fully trust in it. At some point, we open our eyes and find ourselves on this ego emotional roller coaster, and we have no idea how to get off.

> Most of us have experiences throughout life in which we know we are being guided by a higher power. But at some point, we become so enmeshed in the ego and its thought and belief system, that we forget how to access this guidance or fully trust in it. At some point, we open our eyes and find ourselves on this ego emotional roller coaster, and we have no idea how to get off.

We wonder why we feel alone and isolated or why we feel constantly attacked by other people. We wonder why we feel the desire to attack others or ourselves. Again, we find ourselves frightened, lost, and incomplete because of our misidentification with the body, which symbolizes separation, imperfection, and mortality. Most of us don't necessarily feel this way all the time. We may live a pretty good life, but we might have moments that come out of nowhere and can be pretty debilitating. We may feel like a cloud has come over us, and suddenly we find ourselves not trusting life and full of fear. This leads us back to that search for home, our true nature in which we remember that we are all connected, but even more than that, we are all One. We have a deep memory of this but cannot remember how to get back to it.

The good news is, when this ego-self gets out of hand and begins limiting our experience of consciousness, we can then do something to have the best of both worlds. We can get back to experiencing unbounded consciousness in which we experience consciousness without limiting it to the ego *and* we can remember and experience our truest nature as Spirit: whole, perfect, and eternal, even amid this human experience. This is awakening.

ACIM helps to lay new groundwork of thoughts and beliefs, which aid in our remembrance of our true nature as whole, perfect, and eternal and the realization that we are always with God no matter how much the ego makes us think that we are not. Yoga helps to clear out the learned ego thought system and open us back up to unbounded consciousness, pure awareness, and the actual experience of the truth of who and what we really are as perfect creations of God, always in His presence.

In the next chapter we will continue to shine the light within this ego cloud through a further look at our beliefs, until the truth of what we forgot begins to dawn on us slowly but surely.

CHAPTER 4

The Santa Phenomenon

God's peace and joy are yours.
—ACIM W-PI.105.1:1

Growing Distrust

The second crack in my perception of the world was when I first learned the truth about Santa Claus. I wanted to hold on to that magical belief as long as possible. When one of my best friends at the time told me that Santa wasn't real, I couldn't take it. "Your mom must be lying to you."

I convinced myself and my best friend, albeit briefly, that her mom must be lying.

I'll never forget walking into my parents' study to ask them if it was true. Mom was sitting at her desk, paying bills, and Dad was next to her, using his computer.

"Mom, is Santa Claus really real?"

"Yes, Ginger."

"Then why did Erin's mom tell her he wasn't real?"

As Mom started bullshitting about the spirit of Christmas, Dad was behind her, shaking his head that Santa wasn't real.

After listening to Mom's spiel, I asked, "So is he real or not?"

"Yes."

"Then why is Dad shaking his head no?"

Luckily for me, my dad realized that I was way too old to be believing and it couldn't be good for my self-image at school.

I'm pretty sure every kid who ever believed in Santa remembers that achingly painful moment of discovering the truth. That magical yearly event turned into a cold, stark holiday by contrast, devoid of meaning and magic. I was still too young at that point to understand the most magical and meaningful symbolism of Christmas in terms of the birth of the Christ Mind and the generous spirit of St. Nick, despite the attempts made by my mom to explain them to me. All I cared about was that Santa and his magic reindeer weren't landing on my rooftop ever again, and even worse, they never did.

To me, this complete and total letdown about Santa is such an obvious analogy to what most of us go through when the ego takes over and cuts us off from the remembrance of our true nature in Spirit and our underlying connection with each other and with God.

This began a crack in my perception of what was the truth and what was not. A crack that, as painful and baffling as it was at first, led me eventually to be able to have the wide-open mind necessary for the path I was to travel.

Back to my parents' study: "Is the story of Adam and Eve true? Was Jesus real?
Oh no, is the Easter Bunny not real either?"

My mom tried her best to tell me what was true and what was not. But the distrust was already growing, and I felt for the first time that my mom wasn't really convinced herself of what was real and what was not. As with my parents' fighting, learning the truth about Santa deepened the gray that began to color my world. This distrust, however, enabled me to break away from my old, inherited beliefs just enough to be more open to other beliefs that I came across much later in life with ACIM and yoga; beliefs that resonated more deeply within me.

We Must Remember Our True Nature
and How It Came to Be Whole-Perfect-Eternal

Allow common sense to come to you as you listen to the next bit of information. There is a basic belief that you will need to look at for you to understand what your true nature is and for awakening to make sense. For this, we are going to look at some workbook lessons from ACIM:

"I am in the likeness of my Creator. Love created me like itself" (ACIM W-PI. 84.1:7–8).
"God, being Love, is also happiness" (ACIM W-PI.103.2:4).
"Happiness is an attribute of love. It cannot be apart from it. Love has no limits, being everywhere" (ACIM W-PI.103.1:1–2, 4).
"God's peace and joy are yours" (ACIM W-PI.105.1:1).

God is perfect as unconditional love and contains the attributes of unconditional love, such as joy and peace. Therefore, God is all-loving, all-peaceful, and all-joyful.

This is the message that Jesus brought two thousand years ago. This is when, in the Judeo-Christian tradition, the perception of the Godhead changed from the idea of a wrathful, vengeful God that you find in the Old Testament to a loving, forgiving God that Jesus brought to the table.

Here's where we get confused. When we think about God creating us, we automatically jump to the belief that God created us in the body. But the body dies eventually; the self-image we create in this life fades over time after our death. Would God create something that eventually dies?

If God created us in His image as perfection—whether you believe God is a He/She/Divine Source/Cosmic Consciousness—then we must assume that God created us at least initially in *Spirit* as perfection. Spirit would be most similar to what we could all imagine God to be. *Here's where we get confused.* When we think about God creating us, we automatically jump to the belief that God created us in the body. But the body dies eventually; the self-image we create in this life fades over time after our death. Would God create something that eventually dies?

We must wake up to the common-sense belief that *initially* God created us as Spirit, since this is the aspect that is godlike in its eternal nature and perfection. When we focus on God creating us in the body, which we know to be mortal, it *subconsciously* instills a fear of God in us, because we subconsciously think that God is, on some level, allowing us to suffer and die. This is not easy to see at first, but ACIM does a great job in helping us to uncover this fear and eventually see God as all-loving, which takes away the fear of Him allowing us to suffer in any way. ACIM says, "*Spirit* is the Thought of God which He created like Himself. The unified spirit is God's one Son, or Christ." (ACIM C-1.1:3-4)

So God created us, not in the body but in His image, in Spirit as whole, perfect, and eternal, meaning we are all one; perfect in love, peace, and joy; and eternal with no end. If we can agree that God created us in Spirit in His image as whole-perfect-eternal, then how did the form come into existence? How did the body come into existence? How did consciousness come out of pure awareness for us to even be able to experience this separate form? Here is where this belief and our understanding *isn't* so important.

You might believe that God created us as one in Spirit, *and then* He created the body and form that we are experiencing. You might believe that God created us as one in Spirit, and then *we* somehow manifested the form ourselves. You might believe that we are one with God so whether He or we manifested the form is one and the same. This is not important. The most important thing is to believe that God is all-loving and created us *initially* in His image as perfect in Spirit. We will go into another possibility that explains the manifestation of form shortly.

I know a lot of us have a deep belief that God created this world and us in these bodies, and that belief is okay. But no matter what your belief, *how* the form came into existence is not important; *what's important is for us not to identify with the form as our true nature, because the form is impermanent.* Let's say that again. What's important is for us to not identify with the form as our true nature because the form is impermanent. We can still have the utmost regard for the form, but we recognize it as a temporary extension of our experience of consciousness.

What's important is for us to not identify with the form as our true nature because the form is impermanent. We can still have the utmost regard for the form, but we recognize it as a temporary extension of our experience of consciousness.

When we shift our identification of "self" to our truest nature as Spirit, which is perfection, which is eternal, we then realize that all the problems experienced on the level of form can have no negative effect on our truest nature in Spirit. *No-thing* can affect this eternal perfection. This allows us to remain perfectly peaceful, even while entrenched in this human experience. From here, we are then guided through life by Holy Spirit, by our higher self, guided to bring our peace and perfection in Spirit to these worldly problems in the most perfect way we can.

It's not easy to remember our true nature once we have been immersed in the ego's thought system for years and years. Even now, this all may sound crazy, and the ego will try and convince you that this is nonsense and not worth your time. How do we shift our identification to our true nature and grasp these concepts when the thought system we have been working from for years and years is telling us that this is crazy?

Again, we rely on common sense.

A Further Look at Our Beliefs

We have to ask ourselves if this resonates as the truth. A God who is all-loving would not want us to experience even one moment of pain or suffering, dissatisfaction, or unfulfillment. A God who is all-loving would not want us to experience the death of a child, the death of a loved one, or any amount of suffering.

It makes sense that God is calling for us to awaken out of this suffering, out of this misidentification with the ego-self and its thought system. It makes sense that there is an awakening that needs to happen. We can learn to go within in such a way that we feel our deep connection with everyone we've ever loved and will ever love. We can learn to go within in such a way that we catch a glimpse of our true nature and remember our Oneness with God and all of creation. It takes practice to learn how to go within in this way—practice *and* help from above. This practice brings that sacredness back into our everyday lives. It brings us further than simply understanding these beliefs. It brings us into the truth and experience of these beliefs. We are filled with reverence for ourselves and all beings, all of creation. This allows us to live a life in full realization of the bigger picture, as we have more moments of awakening into what yoga calls our truest nature and what ACIM calls Spirit.

How Is God Calling for Us to Awaken?

God knows that on some level, we have forgotten our true nature and are experiencing suffering in many forms. From ACIM's standpoint, God has sent the Holy Spirit, a part of our own Spirit, to awaken us. God is calling to us to awaken through guidance from Holy Spirit in every moment. We only need to learn how to listen.

Within this experience of the false ego-self, the Holy Spirit, our higher self, is putting things in our lives to help us awaken. Here we may be led to a book about awakening or a conversation that opens us up more to the awareness of the love, peace, and joy that is within. We may be led to practices which help us to tune in more deeply to Holy Spirit so that we may be guided in the perfect way for our own awakening.

For me, this makes perfect sense. It's hard to believe in a God who would be okay with some of the pain and suffering that some people go through in life. This is why this belief system makes so much sense to me and resonates as the truth for me. God *is* calling through the Holy Spirit, through our inner guidance, and when we really start trusting in this inner guidance rather than the analytical, thinking mind that ego controls, life begins to shift and change for the better.

ACIM asks the question, "Who chooses hell when it is recognized?" (ACIM C-2.10:5). In other words, why would we choose this hell of the ego-mind when we realize there is a way out? Why would we choose this hell when we realize we are being guided in every moment to awaken by God Himself calling us through our own intuition, through our higher self? Why wouldn't we choose to learn to go within to find the truth of who we are and a Oneness so infinite that it completely wipes out any form of loneliness or sadness from thinking we are separate, imperfect, and mortal?

I was once told that I didn't know what suffering was until I went around the world and saw it with my own eyes. My reply was, "I have seen suffering. I have seen suffering enough for a thousand people, behind my own closed door, behind my own closed eyelids." The truth is, all of us have had our fair share of suffering, and in many cases there never seems a good reason for it. But I can say for myself that as difficult and painful as moments in my life have been before in terms of depression, the Holy Spirit, my guardian angels, God Himself, God within has led me back to the light. I know that no matter what we may have to endure in life, we all have the choice to see differently, to live awake, and to lead an exquisite life by doing so.

For whatever reason I decided to have this experience to begin with, I am sure glad I was finally able to listen enough to be led to a practice that has brought me to where I am now: to be able to remember who I really am as connected and One with *all*. This remembrance allows me to fully enjoy this experience—the good and the bad—while it is still here for me. Knowing beyond a shadow of a doubt that we can never lose anyone or anything that is eternally and infinitely connected to us from within takes the fear out of life and allows us to experience the peace, love, and joy that is our true nature. The trouble is, even though the ego causes suffering, we can become so wrapped up in it that we believe that we would rather be separate. There is a part of the ego-self that convinces us that we enjoy the separation and the competition and drama that comes with it.

How Do We Even Begin to Wake Up?

At this point, you may feel overwhelmed with these concepts, or they may simply sound downright crazy. That's okay; all of us start here. But what can help us to wake up when we don't necessarily believe that there is anything to wake up from or that we *want* to wake up from?

Initially, we can use the contemplative practices (yoga practices) to shift out of the ego's thought system and into what yoga calls our true nature. This is a very relaxed state, in which we actually go beyond the body, beyond the mind, and into our true nature as pure awareness. Guided relaxations are great for taking us into our true nature quite easily. This is where you simply lie down and listen to a guided meditation or relaxation as you let your body and mind relax. This is where we find higher guidance, access our intuition, and find answers that are beyond the thinking mind's ability to do so.

On a plaque on a wall at Kripalu Center for Yoga and Health, there is the following quote from Swami Kripalu about yoga: "The spiritual path I teach ... is not a sectarian creed or point of view. It is performance of skillful actions that lead one to the direct realization to truth. Truth cannot belong to any one race, sect, or nation. It does not recognize such narrow distinctions and makes itself available to the whole world."

Kripalu is saying that these practices lead us to the realization of truth, the truth of who and what we really are. What happens when we start practicing yoga as meditation or movement meditation is that we have an experience of peace. In consistent practice, we experience the essence of our true nature, which naturally takes us out of the ego-self and its thought system.

Once we get acquainted with these experiences, we can then look closely at the ego's thought system and belief system, really study it, and recognize how much it doesn't make sense, because it is in opposition to the truth we are now experiencing through the practice. We begin to see through the ego's thought system, which weakens our identification with the ego-self and strengthens our relationship with our higher self (Holy Spirit) and God. This helps us to begin to lose that ego desire for separation and competition.

If you *can't* believe in a God who is all-loving; if you *can't* believe in a God who is calling for us to awaken out of suffering; if you *can't* believe there is a part of you that wants more than anything for you to *wake up*, then go no further.

For the rest of you, there is a part of ourselves that is trying to wake us up, that wants more than anything for us to just *wake up*. We must remember the truth of who we really are and ensure that we never forget in any moment. If you believe you are eternal Spirit, the effect of that belief is astronomical, and your life will change. What seals the deal is the actual experience of being eternal Spirit, which you will get through the practice of yoga.

As we remember and reconnect with our true nature in Spirit, we are lifted above the impermanence and imperfection of this world and realize that it has no effect on our true nature. This gives us immense freedom and peace, enhancing our ability to be open to our higher guidance as we experience more and more moments in pure awareness, leading us to live deeply peaceful lives and actually drawing more and more of Spirit's peace and perfection into the world of the impermanent.

In the next chapter we will learn the basic yet most important components of yoga that *Choose Spirit Now* (as a tool) is built upon to help us understand the ego so that we can awaken from it.

CHAPTER 5

Choose Spirit Now

All yoga practices are designed to lead one to an experience of being infinite, eternal, and whole. An experience of being infinite, eternal, and whole is beyond a belief that you are infinite, eternal, and whole. The mind can't get there, so at some point you must leap off the mind experience into another realm.

—Devarshi Steven Hartman (2013)

Sometimes It Just Takes Something Else

I read many self-help and spiritual books in my teens and twenties that propelled me forward on my path. I read books my dad had read, my therapist suggested, my teachers recommended. All helped me immensely in their own different ways. All helped me to see how I was coping now with what had gone on as a child.

All of these books were great, but I still had a lot of deep emotional pain that I could not intellectualize my way out of.

Yoga and ACIM—My Spiritual Quest Leading to Truth

Eventually we find a spiritual path that speaks to us so profoundly that we are awakened to the truth that is already in us, and we no longer need to search for what is already there. There are many paths to the truth. I knew when I found mine by the cessation of my suffering, all my worry, insecurities, judgments, and depression, and the ability to remain in a state of peace (most of the time), beyond the chaos of the mind. What I've learned from studying yoga and ACIM and from my own consistent yoga practice is that finding happiness and fulfillment that lasts, finding that peace within beyond the chaos of the mind, *is* possible! This doesn't mean everything is always perfect. But when things come up, I can recognize the ego at work, and it doesn't take me on quite the emotional roller coaster ride it used to.

> This doesn't mean everything is always perfect. But when things come up, I can recognize the ego at work, and it doesn't take me on quite the emotional roller coaster ride it used to.

I used to think enlightenment was for spiritual gurus or cloistered nuns. Now I know that it is a possibility for all of us. We are all spiritual beings, and we are all capable of living awake in this very lifetime. The best reason I can give to you for wanting to understand awakening is how much more you will enjoy your life, your loved ones, and the world around you. *This* is your life; there *is* no dress rehearsal. We *can* get to a point where we can enjoy every moment of it—the seemingly good, the seemingly bad, and everything in between! We can get to a point where we are drawing the light forth form ourselves, our loved ones, and the world around us!

Choose Spirit Now

Choose Spirit Now focuses on us remembering our truest nature as Spirit and therefore reconnecting to our eternal, all-loving, all-peaceful, and all-joyful nature. CSN focuses on strengthening and deepening trust in our higher self that is guiding us in every moment, and, most importantly, guiding us to remember our true nature. This gives us an immense amount of freedom, because now our teacher is our higher self. No more running to find someone to ask your questions about what to do in your life. No more searching for the perfect teacher or book to give you that perfect answer. This does not mean you never speak with others, friends, teachers or therapists, about difficult dilemmas you come across in your life. It can help to have sounding boards to aid in you accessing your intuition. Simply acknowledge that your higher self is constantly guiding you and do everything in your power to tune into that guidance. Many times it leads you to the people in life that will most help you deal with your situation from a Spirit point of view rather than an ego point of view, thus handling the situation in a more awakened state.

Once you open up to your higher self and inner guidance, everything you need to know is within you, and you now can trust that knowledge within. From here, we are guided effortlessly through life, guided to make the most powerful, positive impact on ourselves and the world around us. Living from this remembrance of our true nature and allowing ourselves to be guided from this true nature is "awakening."

Awakening is not some golden trophy awaiting you at the end of a long and arduous journey. It is here for you right here, right now. Each moment gives you an opportunity to live awake. Many people call it the cosmic joke because when you really get "awakening," it is so simple, it makes you laugh for days. As we quit tuning in to the thinking/analyzing/judging mind that the ego-self controls, we allow ourselves to be guided effortlessly throughout life by our intuition which ultimately leads us to the remembrance of our truest nature as Spirit. If you are still having trouble wrapping your brain around these concepts, don't fret. That's what this is all about—undoing the ego's grip, layer by layer, so we can finally *see* clearly.

Three Components of Yoga that CSN is Based Upon

The *Yoga Sutras* say, "Yogic action has three components—discipline, self-study, and orientation toward the goal of pure awareness. It's purposes are to disarm the causes of suffering and achieve integration" (Hartranft 2003, 285). So, here it is right here. According to yoga, we awaken from suffering, awaken from the ego's thought system, by being disciplined enough to study ourselves so that we can understand what's going on with the ego *and* by being disciplined enough to orient ourselves toward the goal of pure awareness (toward the goal of having more and more moments remembering and experiencing our truest nature as Spirit). We orient ourselves toward pure awareness easily through the yoga practices. This takes us out of the ego's thought system automatically and into an experience of our true nature as pure awareness, or Spirit. Yoga practices can include seated meditation, movement meditation, guided meditation, or really *anything* that helps us to awaken to pure awareness.

Choose Spirit Now uses these three components of yogic action to help us move through this process of awakening. Throughout this book, we will be learning aspects of yoga and ACIM, which will help us understand the ego and how to study it within our own lives (self-study). We will be learning what yoga practices do to aid us in shifting from ego-self to our true nature almost effortlessly (orientation toward the goal of pure awareness). And we will be setting an intention to stay disciplined in our self-study and practice until we understand and experience awakening (discipline). Choose Spirit Now aids us in living life awake.

Discipline for Choose Spirit Now

Sankalpa is a Sanskrit word meaning an intention; a resolution to be put into practice; a promise to yourself for your higher good. Think of it as a New Year's resolution.

Take a moment to write your own *sankalpa* to stay committed to your lifelong, moment-by-moment choice to live awake. Set some time aside to write out your own *sankalpa*, and really put some energy behind it. Write it in this book if you have to. This is your intention to stay disciplined and dedicated to live a more peaceful life. This won't take a whole lot of effort, just a keen awareness of how you are living, so that you can make the best choices to live your life awake.

Self-Study or *Svadiyaya*

You may have heard of the eight-limbed path of yoga written about in the *Yoga Sutras*. Self-study, or *svadiyaya* in Sanskrit, is not just considered one of the three components of yogic action, but is also a part of this eight-limbed path. Self-study is one of the yogic internal observances meaning self-observation without judgment. Cope quotes Swami Kripalu: "The major principle in self-observation is that the observer remains neutral and objective" (2006, 135). It's simply to study ourselves as we move through life, but completely without judgment. Throughout this book, we will be using this self-study to shine the light on our ego, to recognize when we are being controlled by it, so that we can continue to see through it more and more.

As we understand the ego and its thought system, we will get better at discerning when the ego is in control. The ego is tricky, with millions of manipulations to get you off the track of awakening, so the self-study aspect of yoga is extremely important and effective. There may be aspects of your own ego-self that you are embarrassed to face, but these ego aspects are not your true nature, so there is absolutely nothing to be ashamed or embarrassed about. Throughout this book, we will go over in great detail what to look out for in our self-study. But remember, all self-study must be *without* judgment! That's what will make this fun and interesting.

Practice (Orientation Toward the Goal of Pure Awareness)

What the mind cannot grasp through self-study, the experience itself through practice will give to the experiencer. The yoga practices work on us in ways beyond our minds' ability to comprehend as long as ego is still in control; this is why they are so important. We will grasp as much as we can through ACIM and yoga principles and philosophy, but at some point, we need the practices to take us beyond the body and beyond the mind to the experience of awakening, to the experience of pure awareness. This is why so many of us fall in love with yoga, because we are being given little gifts of awakening, and most of us don't even realize that when we first begin. All we know is that we feel really good, really peaceful.

Yoga brings us more fully into the body, so we can then go beyond the body. Yoga focuses the mind, so we can then let go of the mind completely. Eventually, during the yoga practice, we go beyond the discomforts of the body and beyond the ego noise of the mind. We awaken within to a place of complete peace, where we begin to feel again our underlying sense of connection with every aspect of creation. This is what yoga calls our true nature, pure awareness of interconnectedness, Oneness.

Devarshi Steven Hartman was one of my teachers at Kripalu for my teacher training. He was a resident at Kripalu back when it was an ashram, with Swami Kripalu as the guru. He says, "All yoga practices are designed to lead one to an experience of being infinite, eternal, and whole. An experience of being infinite, eternal, and whole is beyond a belief that you are infinite, eternal, and whole. The mind can't get there, so at some point you must leap off the mind experience into another realm" (Hartman 2013). Devarshi is a longtime student and excellent teacher of both yoga and ACIM, over thirty years of studying and teaching both. For more information on Steven Hartman, check out his website, *www.stevenhartman.com.*

The practices are what really begin to transform your life! So find some yoga practices you enjoy, either through a local yoga studio, DVDs, or start your own personal practice with what you have already learned in the past. The practices don't have to be difficult. You don't have to be strong or flexible. The best ones are the guided relaxations and meditations in which you simply lie down and relax as you listen. If you find your mind wanders and you cannot completely relax, then that's where the movement meditations will help. These will help you release stress in both mind and body that is inhibiting you from fully relaxing into the guided relaxations and guided meditations.

The practices are simply meant to get you present in your body and focused in your mind, so you can go beyond both body and mind into the experience of your true nature. You can do yoga in bed if you need to! We will go further into what the practice is doing for us in a later chapter, but you don't need to understand this quite yet to reap the full benefits. So go ahead and get started with your practice.

The ego will pull the wool over our eyes again and again. It is up to us to have the discipline and dedication to pick ourselves back up and utilize the self-study and practices to pull the wool out from over our eyes and get back to being awake. Our relationship with our higher self is what will ultimately give us the strength and ability to keep going back to the drawing board over and over again, to stay with the process until we are given the gift of little or no ego.

In the next chapter, we will learn to strengthen our relationship and deepen our trust in our higher self, what ACIM calls Holy Spirit. This will allow our higher self to aid us in working with the ego in more depth and lead us in the most perfect way for each of our own paths to awakening.

CHAPTER 6

Aha Moment with Holy Spirit

No step is lost on this path, no dangers are found, and even a little progress is freedom from fear.
—Krishna speaking to Arjuna,
The Bhagavad Gita (Mascaro 2003, 13)

This Was My Aha Moment

When I first realized that Holy Spirit was the higher self and it spoke to me through my inner guidance, my intuition, it was an amazing aha moment for me. I was already pretty tuned in to my intuition, so learning that my intuition was the Holy Spirit guiding me made me realize that I should really listen up. Understanding that Holy Spirit is the higher self made it more reachable. It was no longer some mysterious aspect of the Trinity that I as a human being was not good enough to even look at.

Now it was reachable, it was accessible, and that's the key. God knew we could get caught up in this ego mind-set and get stuck, so He speaks to us through the Holy Spirit, via our intuition. He is giving us unlimited guidance to awaken out of the ego-self in every moment, leading us to live a life awake and spiritually fulfilled. This makes life a whole different ball of wax. It's so simple; it seems too easy. All we need to do is to learn to tune in to and trust in our own intuition. Yoga and *A Course in Miracles* helps us do just that. Now we can live an exquisite life as we listen to our higher self's guidance and remember in every moment that nothing in this world can alter our true nature as whole, perfect, and eternal.

On some level we wanted to have this human experience. Once we become immersed in the ego-self and experience suffering, our higher self does its best to remind us of our true nature so that we can *fully enjoy* this human experience while we have it. When I say "fully enjoy", I mean *fully enjoy* the good, the bad, and everything in between. We can do this when we really get that *nothing* can alter our true nature.

> Once we become immersed in the ego-self and experience suffering, our higher self does its best to remind us of our true nature so that we can *fully enjoy* this human experience while we have it. When I say "fully enjoy", I mean *fully enjoy* the good, the bad, and everything in between. We can do this when we really get that *nothing* can alter our true nature.

When I first came upon the term "Holy Spirit" in ACIM, I felt some aversion to it. I experienced ego resistance to a term on which I was still placing past association. It took a little time, but finally I was able to clear all that past association and meaning out and have this new understanding of Holy Spirit as my higher self, guiding me through my intuition, my inner guidance. When I really got this, the term "Holy Spirit" no longer brought up this aversion. Now it brings up a warm feeling, as I recognize it as the highest part of myself, not something separate or inaccessible.

> Follow your intuition, and you are following God's call to awaken. Follow your intuition, and you are making the most powerful, positive impact on your life, the lives around you, and the world around you as well.

Follow your intuition, and you are following God's call to awaken. Follow your intuition, and you are making the most powerful, positive impact on your life, the lives around you, and the world around you as well. How amazing is that!

Makes you want to tune in, doesn't it?

Strengthening Relationship with Holy Spirit

Every morning, you can connect with Holy Spirit, your higher self, with a simple intention. You can find this morning meditation on *ChooseSpiritNow.com*:

> Holy Spirit please help guide me throughout my day today. Help me to stay connected to you so that I may be tuned into your guidance through my own intuition. I recognize you as part of my own eternal Spirit that I share with every aspect of creation. Help me to be open to seeing little signs throughout my day today reminding me of my peaceful, eternal nature in Spirit- forever connected to you and all of creation through God. As I connect with others throughout my day help me to share this experience of being guided, connected, and peaceful, with whomever I meet, without having to say a word. Help me to Choose Spirit Now in every situation that may come about reminding myself to be guided by Spirit, rather than controlled by the ego. Namaste.

Write down any intuitive feelings you may begin having as you get in the habit of setting this intention every morning. Ask for synchronicities, which are meaningful coincidences, throughout your day. In the morning, when I connect with Holy Spirit, I ask for those little signs to remind me to stay connected. Every day that I ask, I get them; I am always blown away by what I get. I will see a sign that I know is a gift from my higher self, reminding me to stay the path, reminding me of my true nature as eternal Spirit, and it always makes me smile.

As your relationship with your higher self strengthens, notice if you begin to feel as if you are being guided effortlessly through life. Remember, guidance from Holy Spirit will instill peace and calm in the mind.

Asking for Guidance for Something Specific

If I am trying to make a decision and the thought of one option causes me stress and anxiety, while the thought of the other option makes me feel calm and peaceful inside, then I know which option my intuition is guiding me toward. It's not always this easy. Sometimes the best decision for you will still cause discomfort. This is where the yoga practice can help you distinguish between ego manipulating you and Spirit guiding you.

If you ask for guidance and are not getting a concrete answer, it doesn't mean that Holy Spirit isn't listening. It means that not all the information is out on the table. So you may need to wait a few days, maybe a week, maybe a month. Once that information comes in, you know what decision will be best for you. Just because you are not getting an immediate answer for guidance does not mean that Holy Spirit is off on a smoke break! More likely, not all the information is on the table, and you are not meant to make this decision at this point in time. Keep up with consistent practice to keep your mind as clear as possible and open to hearing the guidance when it comes.

Heads Up!

As we turn the spotlight on the ego-self, the more manipulative, conniving, and downright mean it can become. It will feel like it's saying to you, "I'm going to take you down!" Don't worry, though. As Jesus made it past the temptations of the ego on his forty-day, forty-night trek through the desert, we can too with the help of the Holy Spirit. That's why trust in our relationship with our higher self is so important! It's not that the ego-self is evil (although it certainly can seem so at times), it just knows that it is being undone which triggers fear and a subsequent "fight" for its ego-life. We still have a deep belief that this ego-self is the real us and so as we undo the ego and let go of this false self, we fear we might be destroying ourselves at the same time.

Resistance to Concepts

Spirituality is our right as eternal Spirit. Don't allow the ego to keep you from awakening, to keep you from a life of absolute spiritual fulfillment, to keep you from a life of peace and joy and love. The ego will use every trick in the book to make you think this sounds crazy; that living a life of lasting fulfillment is impossible; that you, on some level, deserve to suffer; and that the last thing you have time for is to get involved in some "holy-roller shenanigans"!

"I've got real responsibilities to take care of, for goodness' sake. I've got kids, bills, and Aunt Erma to take care of! I live in the real world!" Sound familiar?

Once all this starts to sink in, you will realize that it is the sanest thing you've heard in your lifetime. This new perspective is uncomfortable for the ego because it leads to its undoing, so there will be an initial discomfort as the ego resists. As you begin developing more trust in your higher self guiding you through your intuition, you will more easily recognize this ego-resistance for what it is and be able to prevent it from tricking you out of your awakening.

My Own Resistance

I had a lot of resistance to my own initial introduction to *A Course in Miracles* concepts. The Christian terminology from the Course at first rubbed me the wrong way.

I was raised Catholic, so on one level, I felt like the Course was some form of irreverence, in that it was saying that it was Jesus' teachings and it spoke of the Holy Spirit, and yet it wasn't the Bible. On another level, I had distanced myself from Christianity at this point, so these terms were difficult to re-assimilate. On top of all that, I didn't want to end up sounding like a holy roller. When you start talking about Jesus and the Holy Spirit all the time, you don't want your friends to start pointing at you and saying, "Oh my God, what has happened to her?"

But as I kept facing the same small dissatisfactions in life, the same small moments of having the blues, the same small moments of kicking myself for something stupid I did, and the same big fears of losing loved ones, I realized that maybe I was ready to try a different way of looking at things.

I want to share a passage from the Bhagavad Gita, which is a very old Indian poem. In this poem, Krishna, who is God, is speaking to a man named Arjuna. He says the following about yoga: "No step is lost on this path, no dangers are found, and even a little progress is freedom from fear" (Mascaro 2003, 13). I love this passage. Allow it to be a reminder that there is nothing to fear with Course or yogic principles.

Choose Spirit Now is all about a connection with your higher self, the loving and forgiving teachings of Jesus, and a God, a Divine Presence that only wants happiness and joy for us in every moment. It's about clarifying beliefs that make real sense, rather than continuing to believe in the ego's thought system based on fear and separation. It's about a yogic practice that is thousands of years old, which can truly help us bridge the gap between understanding principles of awakening and actually experiencing this awakening right here, right now.

Our Choice

we have a choice to misidentify our *self* with the body and the self-image we build in life and then experience the subsequent fear, guilt, insecurity, and misery that this misidentification causes; or we can Choose Spirit Now and remember our truest nature as eternal, peaceful Spirit and experience the subsequent love, peace, and joy this correct identification brings.

So it comes down to this: we have a choice to misidentify our *self* with the body and the self-image we build in life and then experience the subsequent fear, guilt, insecurity, and misery that this misidentification causes; or we can Choose Spirit Now and remember our truest nature as eternal, peaceful Spirit and experience the subsequent love, peace, and joy this correct identification brings. We have a choice to have our mind controlled by the ego-self and its thought system or to have our mind guided by Spirit. We have a choice to live in dissatisfaction as we constantly analyze and think our way through life or to live in absolute spiritual fulfillment, trusting in the guidance from our higher self, which leads us in the most perfect way for ourselves and all of creation.

And that's what Choose Spirit Now is all about—understanding this choice and getting us to a place in life where we can even slow down enough to be able to make that choice.

So here's the question: are you ready to take responsibility for the life you want to live and draw more peace and positive transformation into your life, the lives around you, and the world around you as well?

Are you ready to *Choose Spirit Now*?

PART II

Thinning Out and Rising Above the Ego Cloud

CHAPTER 7

Step 1 to Awakening

When the components of yoga are practiced, impurities dwindle; then the light of understanding can shine forth, illuminating the way to discriminative awareness.
—Yoga Sutra 28 (Hartranft 2003, 286).

Witness Consciousness

Witness consciousness is a yogic term describing the aspect of our consciousness in which we begin noticing ourselves living immersed in the ego-self. In witness consciousness we become *conscious* of our consciousness attributing our "self" to the ego thoughts, beliefs, judgments, and self-image. A teacher once likened living in the ego to having an octopus stuck on your face and you don't even know it. At some point, the octopus begins to detach, and we realize that we have been walking around with this octopus suctioned to our face, and it's unbelievable.

In witness consciousness we become *conscious* of our consciousness attributing our "self" to the ego thoughts, beliefs, judgments, and self-image.

Because we are living so immersed in the ego-self and its thought system, it can be difficult to recognize witness consciousness initially. It's like tuning in to a different radio frequency in our mind. Once we slow down enough to recognize witness consciousness, then we can begin to grasp what the ego's thought system is and notice it at work in our minds as we non-judgmentally observe it. This non-judgmental observance of the ego-self and its thought system through witness consciousness is the self-study.

We will go deeper into what witness consciousness is and what can be accomplished from it, but for now, our higher self utilizes this state of consciousness for us to begin the steps to awakening.

Ego as Emotion from Thoughts, Beliefs, and
Judgments about the Past and the Future

One way to grasp how much you may live with ego controlling the mind is by looking at how the ego is tied into the past and the future. If you are like most of us, you spend most of your day thinking—about the past and about the future. The ego can only exist in the past and the future, not the present, because it consists only of thoughts, beliefs, and subsequent emotions that are based on experience of the past and anticipated experience of the future. When we think about how much time we spend thinking and worrying about the past or thinking and worrying about the future, we realize how often we are living with ego controlling the mind.

When we are stuck in this ego-self, thinking about the past or the future, we then have emotional energy that comes up in relation to these thoughts, beliefs, and judgments. If we allow ourselves to feel these emotions fully, then we can be done with them (until the next thought, belief, and judgment stirs them back up). But most of us resist these emotions because we anticipate them to be too painful, so we learn to control the emotions and stuff them down. This resistance then causes more anxiety, worry, and stress, because we are not allowing ourselves to express this emotional energy and let it out. Instead, it gets trapped in our being with nothing to do but wreak havoc as we continue to harp on whatever thoughts, beliefs, and judgments are causing the emotion to begin with.

Let's take a moment to look at emotions and how they relate to thoughts, beliefs, and judgments from the past and future. When we feel worried, we are usually worried about something that might happen in the future, based on something that happened in the past. When we feel anxious, we are usually anxious about something that might happen in the future, based on something that happened in the past. When we are fearful, we are usually fearful about the future, based on something that happened in the past. When we feel guilt, sadness, or anger, we are usually feeling it for something that happened in the past or something that might happen in the future. It's all tied into the past and the future.

In a later chapter, we will go over how to fully experience the emotional energy so we can let it go. Most importantly, we will learn how to undo the ego-self that is causing these ego emotions to begin with. As we continue to be immersed in the ego's thought system, it is important to learn to let go of the ego emotion as it comes, but we also have to get to the root of the problem. We must learn to change our thoughts, beliefs, and judgments to more positive ones, but  more importantly we can learn to shift ourselves out of this thought system altogether, back into pure awareness. This takes the root of the problem out of the equation completely.

We must learn to change our thoughts, beliefs, and judgments to more positive ones, but more importantly we can learn to shift ourselves out of this thought system altogether, back into pure awareness.

The ego will distract you with a million different thoughts and subsequent feelings that prevent you from awakening, from experiencing the joy and peace that is here for you right here and now in the present moment. ACIM asks, "What better example could there be of the ego's maxim, "Seek but do not find"?" (ACIM T-16.V.6:5). We try our best to find our peace, joy, and wholeness again. The problem is, we are still working with a mind that is under the ego's control, which is so noisy and chaotic that it distracts us from searching right behind it, within our own awareness for what we are truly looking for. Instead, we are constantly looking outside of ourselves for this peace, joy, and wholeness in all sorts of different ways, but because of this, our search continuously falls short. The ego-self and its thought system prevents us from grasping the simplicity of getting quiet and looking within, where happiness and completion are a God-given part of us.

Step 1 to Awakening: Begin to Live
Consciously Observing the Ego-Self

Part of the first step to awakening is simply to understand what it is that we are awakening from. So, step 1 to awakening is all about beginning to understand the ego and its thought system, so that we can begin studying and observing it. In step 1, when thoughts, beliefs, and judgments arise in our mind, we recognize them as part of this ego mental construct that we have built up around us. Now, when any subsequent emotions arise, we immediately recognize the ego-self and its thought and belief system as the cause. As we begin to simply recognize our thoughts, judgments, and beliefs as part of the ego, the subsequent emotions that these cause have less and less of an effect on us. In step 1, we begin to recognize this witness consciousness state of mind, in which we can observe ourselves living immersed in this made-up ego mental construct.

This is the beginning of a new way of seeing!

This might sound complicated, but it's really a simple shift that happens within your consciousness, as you draw awareness to (recognize) an observer (witness consciousness) inside of you that is separate from all the thoughts going on in your head (ego-self). There is an observer behind all of the chaos in the mind that is not getting wrapped up in the thoughts and the subsequent feelings. This observant state is ever present and peaceful and is used by your higher self, to eventually lead you all the way to a fully awakened state. This fully awakened state is even beyond the observant state and is what yoga calls pure awareness and what ACIM calls Spirit.

Ego as a Cloud Surrounding Us

The first step to "awakening" is simply realizing that we are immersed in the ego's thought system to begin with, like a cloud constantly surrounding us, and then to begin studying it non-judgmentally. This isn't always easy to do. It's like telling someone they have microscopic organisms all over their body. It seems unbelievable at first, until you pull out the microscope and see them all moving around. Fortunately, as we become aware of the ego's thought system and shine the light of self-study onto it, the entire mental construct which has been built out of this ego thought system begins to fade and disappear. This mental construct prevents us from being present with what is happening around us, so once it begins to disassemble, being present and living awake becomes a whole lot easier.

In this first step, we are beginning to poke our head out of the cloud of ego thoughts and beliefs, so we can then turn our awareness onto this cloud and look at it as something separate, not as our true nature. We have misidentified ourselves so completely with the ego-self that most of us begin to believe we are our thoughts, beliefs, and judgments. We believe we are that voice in our head constantly building us up to be better than others or tearing us down, making us feel worthless. We have become so immersed in the ego that we begin to believe this cloud surrounding us is a part of who we are. We must begin to see that we are not these thoughts, beliefs, and judgments or the subsequent emotions they cause. This ego cloud is not a part of us but something separate that we *can* be led out of.

We may begin to recognize another voice, quiet but full of patience, strength, and peace—a voice for God, our higher self, Holy Spirit; a voice here to lead us out of the ego-self and its thought system, out of this ego cloud surrounding us. Eventually, we begin to notice the difference between our higher self and this ego cloud. We begin to see (some call this the third eye opening) that we can awaken out of this ego cloud, that it is not a true part of us. And this is a *huge* step!

Discernment vs. Judgment

In step 1, we establish witness consciousness, that aspect of consciousness our higher self initially utilizes to non-judgmentally observe ourselves living immersed in the ego. ACIM calls this "discernment" of the ego at work in our lives and the lives of others, *but not judgment.* Judgment represents the ego's thought system at work again and Yoga and ACIM both recognize the importance of keeping judgment out of this process. You can discern and witness ego without labeling it good or bad or having a subsequent feeling about it. Judgment is the backbone of the ego mental construct and therefore an extremely hard habit to break, so when you find yourself making a judgment about what you are witnessing, simply notice and then let the judgment go. As you practice letting this judgment go without making a big deal out of it, it will get easier and easier to break this habit. This is an extremely important goal of witness consciousness because as we draw our awareness to these judgments and let them go, we are dismantling the ego's backbone.

This is an extremely important goal of witness consciousness because as we draw our awareness to these judgments and let them go, we are dismantling the ego's backbone.

Yoga and ACIM give us a process to slow down enough in body and mind to begin noticing this witness consciousness aspect in which we are able to discern and observe the ego. In chapter 2 of the *Yoga Sutras,* sutra 28, it says, "When the components of yoga are practiced, [remember the components as discipline, self-study, and orientation toward the goal of pure awareness] impurities dwindle; then the light of understanding can shine forth, illuminating the way to discriminative awareness" (Hartranft 2003, 286). This "discriminative awareness" is the same as witness consciousness, in which we are now able to witness (or discern) the ego working in our lives. As we practice these components of yoga as discipline, self-study, and practice, we establish witness consciousness from which we are able to discern the ego more easily.

True Nature as Spirit: Whole-Perfect-Eternal

Another part of the first step to awakening is understanding what it is that we are trying to wake up *to*. In our true nature as Spirit, we are whole, perfect, and eternal. Perfect in peace, unconditional love, and abundant joy, created in God's image. We are wholly connected with all of creation; eternal with no end.

We may not be able to remain awake in our true nature for long, but we can bring the best of our true nature into everyday life by remembering it as we continue to establish witness consciousness, tap into unbounded consciousness, and allow Holy Spirit to guide us from there. When Spirit is guiding the mind, we feel calm, quiet, peaceful, still, joyful, happy, and unconditionally loving. We are fully in the present moment, fully in the experience of life with absolutely no resistance to the present. The Spirit's motto, according to ACIM, is

"Seek and you will find" (ACIM T-12.IV.4:5). When we begin this path to awakening we begin to realize the importance of implementing certain practices into our lives to help us to remember our true nature and actually shift into the experience of our true nature as often as possible. Now we can remain completely tuned into our guidance from Spirit, from our higher self. This leads us to live an exquisite life as we draw more peace and positive transformation into it.

I'll never forget the moment I realized my concept of God was changing. I'll never forget standing in the shower and beginning to cry as I realized that I no longer saw God as this old man who was comforting but elusive. I was beginning to conceptualize God as a feeling or an experience—an experience of complete love, peace, joy, and harmony that dapples our lives from time to time. An experience that was beginning to show up more and more for me. A part of me grieved the loss of the concept of God as a father figure that day. However, this new concept allowed me to detach even further from overly attributing my *self* with my own body and self-image. It allowed me to begin seeing my *self* more easily as something beyond just an image of the human body, an essence that is not form, yet is the underlying connection between all form. This change in your conception of God isn't a necessity but may happen over time. I still sense God as a loving, parental figure, but not in the same literal sense that I did before.

Our Mind

We are not our mind. The mind is a tool that is used for consciousness but it can be influenced by ego or Spirit. When ego is influencing the mind, we say that ego is controlling the mind, because ego uses the mind to manipulate us, control us, and immerse us into its belief system of separation. Here the ego is limiting consciousness. When Spirit is influencing the mind, we say that Spirit is guiding the mind, because Spirit is guiding us to go beyond filtering everything in life through the ego and get back into the joyful experience of life as we remember our true nature. Here Spirit is expanding consciousness back to that unbounded consciousness we experienced as young children.

Spiritual Growth vs. Spiritual Awakening

Spiritual growth is the idea that we are not already perfect in Spirit and somehow need to "grow" in this life to attain that perfection spiritually. This way of looking at things, although it means well, can accidentally facilitate ego controlling the mind. This idea of "spiritual growth" can cause us to berate ourselves for not being spiritually mature and drive ourselves to grow more spiritually, but it is all ego-based, because only the ego is imperfect and is striving for that perfection. This idea can lead to guilt for not being "perfect," which can send us back on a downward spiral in the ego's thought system. Overall, this causes us to build more ego, rather than clear out more ego.

> We need to awaken from the ego-self, forged by our human experience, in order to remember our perfection in Spirit. So rather than thinking of it as spiritual growth, think of it as a clearing out of the ego: all the learned thoughts, behaviors, patterns, habits, and so on that are now clouding our remembrance of our perfection. This is spiritual awakening!

According to ACIM and yoga, the Spirit has been created in perfection, so there is no need for the Spirit to grow. This is great news! We need to awaken from the ego-self, forged by our human experience, in order to remember our perfection in Spirit. So rather than thinking of it as spiritual growth, think of it as a clearing out of the ego: all the learned thoughts, behaviors, patterns, habits, and so on that are now clouding our remembrance of our perfection. This is spiritual awakening!

Soul vs. Spirit

Where does the soul come in?

We are talking about being whole, perfect, and eternal in Spirit, but what about the soul? The soul has that quality of being individual. I've got a soul; you've got a soul. How can we say that Spirit is whole, connected, when we have these individual souls? Are souls different from Spirit?

In yoga, there's a term called *samskaras*. These are deep impressions from life that have had such an impact on us that they get embedded in our subconscious. Samskaras are an extensive part of the ego-self we build over time. They can come back up automatically when a particular situation or circumstance arises that resembles in any way the circumstance in the past in which these deep impressions were first formed. For instance, if you had a verbally abusive parent who told you that you were worthless every time you made a bad grade in school, you probably have deep impressions of feeling worthless and inadequate. As an adult, anytime your boss gives you a suggestion at work, you might automatically go into feelings of inadequacy and worthlessness, even if the suggestion was well spoken and well intended.

We'll get further into *samskaras* in a later chapter; these deep impressions can be positive, negative, or neutral. We remember these deep impressions subconsciously, to help us assimilate the world and what's happening around us, but certain ones can end up preventing us from experiencing life fully.

There is another term in yoga called *vasanas*. These are the even deeper impressions that we actually take with us when we leave the body. They have been so deeply embedded that they actually stay with us as we move out of the body or even into another lifetime, if you believe in reincarnation. They can also be positive, negative, or neutral. You can think of the soul as the part of the spirit that holds on to *vasanas*, which gives each soul a sense of individuality. Each soul has deep impressions stored from that lifetime or countless lifetimes.

Spirit as whole-perfect-eternal is all the collective souls together without the *vasanas* attached to them. When you truly awaken to Oneness in Spirit, you can think of it as all the collective souls together, but now we are experiencing true Oneness, because we have let go of all our *vasanas*, our deeply embedded impressions. We can learn to detach from these impressions so we can experience Oneness of Spirit more easily.

Here's the kicker. We can drop through the *samskaras* and

> Here's the kicker. We can drop through the *samskaras* and *vasanas* into this Oneness of Spirit within the experience of the body, within the experience of still being attached to these deep impressions! They don't change our Oneness of Spirit; they simply cloud our experience of it.

vasanas into this Oneness of Spirit within the experience of the body, within the experience of still being attached to these deep impressions! They don't change our Oneness of Spirit; they simply cloud our experience of it. So, just like a cloudy day, there may be moments of complete realization of Oneness, and then (BAM!) a cloud comes, and you are back in your habitual patterning and impressions. We are not reliant on every single person detaching from their *vasanas* in order to experience Oneness of Spirit. Oneness of Spirit *cannot be altered*, but the *experience* of Oneness of Spirit can be altered by whether or not there is a cloud of *vasana* overlying it. This is great news! We don't have to wait until we die or until we've lived enough lifetimes to detach enough to experience this. We don't have to wait for everyone else to awaken or meditate two hours a day for thirty years before we catch a glimpse of this Oneness.

We can experience this Oneness of Spirit *right now* and draw the peace and joy which constitutes this experience back in to our daily lives. This is the golden trophy: to be able to experience our true nature *within* the experience of life! Yoga and ACIM shows us how to do this!

In the next chapter, we will go over what is actually happening when you have a moment of awakening and show the similarities between yoga and ACIM in explaining this process.

CHAPTER 8

Awakening According to Yoga and ACIM

Take the first step in faith, you don't have to see the whole
staircase, just take the first step.
—Martin Luther King, Jr. (*www.brainyquote.com,* 2001)

This chapter gives an overview of what is happening in a moment
of awakening. Awakening is not some singular event and that's it.
For most of us we have moments of awakening strung delightfully
throughout our lives. Awakening is simply a moment of remembering.
When we can better understand these moments and the simplicity yet
magnitude of what is happening, we can more easily recognize them
in our own lives as well as set ourselves up for even more of them fairly
easily. I have outlined the process in steps but in reality most of them
happen simultaneously.

Awakening According to Yoga

Once I read ACIM I realized that some of the same terms it used to
describe what happens as we awaken from the ego (or shift from limited
consciousness to pure awareness) were almost identical to the terms
used in yoga for the same process. I will go through the process of both
and then show them side by side. Here is an outline of the process of
awakening that I have come up with based on yogic philosophy and
the *Yoga Sutras*:

1. Practice
2. Witness consciousness
3. Become present
4. Mind quiets
5. Shift out of ego
6. Illumined mind
7. Clear seeing
8. See past the illusion to the truth
9. No more projection
10. Experience our true nature as pure awareness leading to living a life awake

The first 9 steps are dealing with consciousness. Steps one through nine are what happens as we shift from ego-consciousness to witness consciousness to unbounded consciousness. Steps two through nine are happening simultaneously. Step ten is what happens when we shift out of consciousness altogether into pure awareness.

When we *practice* (step 1) yoga as seated meditation or movement meditation (the yoga poses you are familiar with, such as triangle pose), we focus the mind on the breath and the poses we are coming into. "Lengthen the crown of the head toward the sky as you sink your sitz bones into the Earth."As we train the mind on the breath and the details of the pose, we take our mind out of its habitual way of thinking and analyzing and shift into *witness consciousness* (step 2). Witness consciousness is a state from which we begin to live awake. From witness consciousness two things can happen: we can pause here in this observant state and utilize the yogic self-study to observe our ego patterning more closely (something we will get more into in a later chapter); or we can rise out of consciousness entirely.

Shearer translates the second yoga sutra, "Yoga is the settling of the mind into silence." (Shearer 1982, 90) As we experience witness consciousness we *become present* (step 3) and the *mind quiets* (step 4). This automatically *shifts us out of the ego* (step 5), because the ego can only exist in the unsettled mind with thoughts and judgments based on the past and anticipation of the future. Now we shift from ego-consciousness to unbounded consciousness and experience what yoga calls *illumined mind* (step 6).

From illumined mind we experience *clear seeing* (step 7). Cope lists one of the characteristics of Illumined Mind in The Wisdom of Yoga as, "Perceives the interconnectedness of all created things." (Cope 2006, 80) Here we are able to *see past the illusion* (step 8 part 1). The illusion is our experience of the world through the ego-self through which we are unable to see our interconnectedness. (We will go more into what the illusion is in the next chapter.) Sutra 47 in chapter 1 says, "But on refinement of the fourth stage of absorption, there is the dawning of the spiritual light of the Self." (Shearer 1982, 98) As we are able to see past the illusion we begin *to see the truth* (step 8 part 2) of who and what we really are as Spirit.

Now *there can be no more projection* (step 9) because we have shifted out of ego-consciousness and therefore there is no ego-self (with all of its thoughts, beliefs, judgments, and subsequent ego emotions) to project. (We will go more deeply into projection in a later chapter.) At this stage of the process we can easily step out of consciousness altogether (ego, witness, and even unbounded) and *experience our true nature as pure awareness* (step 10), or what we call Spirit.

I often say in my yoga classes that yoga brings us more fully into the body so that we can then go beyond the body and yoga focuses the mind so that we can then go beyond the mind. Through the practice of yoga we move beyond the body, beyond the mind, and into an experience of Spirit, or pure awareness. The last sutra says, "Freedom is at hand when the fundamental qualities of nature, each of their transformations witnessed at the moment of its inception, are recognized as irrelevant to pure awareness; it stands alone, grounded in its very nature, the power of pure seeing. That is all." (Hartranft 2003, 292)

The more we practice the easier it becomes to live life awake. Living life awake means we are having more and more of these moments of full awakening, but most importantly, when we are back to experiencing consciousness we are resting more and more in witness consciousness and unbounded consciousness, rather than strictly ego-consciousness. Here we are able to continue studying and observing the ego, but, most importantly, we remember the truth of who and what we really are as perfect creations of God always in His presence, even amid the human experience.

Awakening According to ACIM

Here is an outline of the process of awakening that I have come up with
based on ACIM. Again, the first 9 steps are dealing with consciousness.
Steps two through nine are happening simultaneously. Step ten is what
happens when we shift out of consciousness altogether into Spirit.

1. Readings/workbook lessons
2. Connect with Holy Spirit
3. Come into the holy instant
4. Mind quiets
5. Shift out of ego
6. Spirit guiding the mind
7. Christ Vision
8. See past the illusion to the truth (miracle)
9. No more projection
10. Experience our true nature as Spirit leads to living the happy
    dream

In the preface of the Course written by Helen Schucman it states,
"The curriculum the Course proposes is carefully conceived and is
explained, step by step, at both the theoretical and practical levels. It
emphasizes application rather than theory, and experience rather than
theology. It specifically states that "a universal theology is impossible,
but a universal experience is not only possible, but necessary" (Manual,
p.77) Although Christian in statement, the Course deals with universal
spiritual themes. It emphasizes that it is but one version of the universal
curriculum. There are many others, this one differing from them only
in form. They all lead to God in the end." (ACIM Preface.viii-ix) This
idea that the course emphasizes *experience* and *application* is what makes
it so similar to yoga which also emphasizes experience and application
through the practice.

The Course workbook states, "The first step is to read the text and
practice the daily workbook lessons. It is the purpose of this workbook
to train your mind to think along the lines the text sets forth." (ACIM
W-In.1:4)

Some of the ideas in the *workbook lessons* (step 1) are meant to be
focused on for five minutes or so, several times a day. This not only

introduces the mind to these teachings but it also takes the mind out of its habitual way of thinking and analyzing by focusing the mind on a particular idea. As the mind becomes more focused, this allows us to *connect with Holy Spirit* (step 2), our higher self. The yoga equivalent to this step is witness consciousness, in which we begin to notice the observer within. This knowledge of yoga really helped me to understand that this connection with Holy Spirit is made simple by noticing the observer within which Holy Spirit uses initially to connect with us.

Once we connect with Holy Spirit this automatically takes us into the *holy instant* (step 3). The holy instant is the same thing as the present moment in which time holds no meaning because there is only now. The Course says, "You look upon each holy instant as a different point in time. It never changes. All that it ever held or will ever hold is here right now. The past takes nothing from it, and the future will add no more. Here, then, is everything." (ACIM T-20.V.6:1-5)

Reading the teachings of the Course begins to free the mind from the limitations the ego has built around it which *quiets the mind* (step 4) and automatically *shifts us out of the ego* (step 5). Now we can tune into *Holy Spirit guiding the mind* (step 6) which enables us to see with *Christ Vision* (step 7). (ACIM T-28.I.11:1) Now we are able to experience the miracle—a shift in our perception. The miracle enables us to *see through the illusion* (step 8 part 1), our experience of the world through the ego-self, and be *open to experiencing the truth* (step 8 part 2) of who and what we really are as One in Spirit. The Course says, "The miracle comes quietly into the mind that stops an instant and is still." Now there is *no more projection* (step 9) because we no longer have this illusion of ego thoughts and fears to project onto others. The Course says, "Release your brothers from the slavery of their illusions by forgiving them for the illusions you perceive in them." (ACIM T-16.VII.9:5)

Now we can *experience our true nature as Spirit* (step 10) and live what ACIM calls *the happy dream*. This is that blissful state where we are *in* the experience of life. In the happy dream we experience the best of both worlds, we remember our truest nature in Spirit even amid the human experience. This is possible here in this lifetime. It's possible right now! The Course says, "You can lose sight of Oneness, but can not make sacrifice of its reality. Nor can you lose what you would sacrifice, nor keep the Holy Spirit from His task of showing you that it has not been lost." (ACIM T-26.I.6:1-2) "Heaven is not a place nor a condition. It is merely an awareness of perfect Oneness, and the knowledge that there is nothing else; nothing outside this Oneness, and nothing else within." (ACIM T-18.VI.1.5-6) Wow. Here the Course is saying that when we remember the truth of our Oneness in a moment of awakening, we are actually experiencing heaven! What could be a better reason to make living life awake a priority?

When I was in my early twenties, I read a book by Sylvia Browne called *Life on the Other Side.* Sylvia Browne is a psychic medium. In the book, she explains what happens when we die. She says we go to a place that is like heaven on Earth, where everything is perfect. The weather is perfect. The Akashic Records are there, in which you can look up anything that has ever happened. She says you can stay here as long as you like, you can reincarnate and come back to Earth, or you can eventually join back with God. When I read this in my twenties, I thought, *Ugh, join back with God? Why would I want to do that? I like being me. I like being Ginger. I want to be me as long as possible.* Joining back with God did not sound like anything I would want to do.

Then in my thirties, I really started studying the ego and began to understand the self-image as being a false sense of self. I realized that in my twenties, I was so attached to my ego self-image as Ginger, with my particular family and my particular life, that joining back with God seemed scary. I felt like I would lose my sense of self, my family and loved ones. What I've realized now is that as we first begin undoing our false sense of self as ego, it is scary, and it does seem like we are losing something. However, once we keep moving forward, at some point we realize that the fear of loss was simply another ego trick to keep us immersed in its thought system.

When you can let go of that false self-image and begin seeing through everyone else's false self-image, it is the most amazing, wonderful experience ever. Now you are seeing yourself and everyone as the light, love, peace, and joy in which we were created as One by God. Once you realize this, you realize that there was nothing to fear in the first place, because the false self-image pales in comparison to what we are together in our true nature as eternal Spirit. What I've realized is that "joining back with God" doesn't mean we go anywhere or leave anyone. It's as simple as being able to see clearly, see the miracle, and awaken to the truth that we are already joined with God, and nothing can change that.

This can be awakened to, within the experience of the body! It's as simple as allowing the ego cloud to dissolve and reveal our Oneness with each other, with all of creation, and with God Himself. We can awaken and live the most wonderful life because of it. It

> What I've realized is that "joining back with God" doesn't mean we go anywhere or leave anyone. It's as simple as being able to see clearly, see the miracle, and awaken to the truth that we are *already* joined with God, and nothing can change that.

doesn't mean you don't experience the ego at all. If you still want to experience the ego, you can by simply ducking your head back beneath the cloud. The difference now is that when you are awake, if you duck your head back down and experience the ego, you know full well that

it is the ego and not your true nature. You know full well that you can poke your head back out of that ego cloud at any time.

In the beginning, you may still have moments of being drawn down into the ego's thought and belief system and the

> In the beginning, you may still have moments of being drawn down into the ego's thought and belief system and the subsequent ego emotion, but it won't draw you in completely. You will still remember the truth of who you are through that emotion and can actually enjoy watching yourself experience this emotion, knowing that it does nothing to lessen your Spirit. How exciting!

subsequent ego emotion, but it won't draw you in completely. You will still remember the truth of who you are through that emotion and can actually enjoy watching yourself experience this emotion, knowing that it does nothing to lessen your Spirit. How exciting!

Yoga and ACIM Side by Side

1. The *practice* in yoga is equivalent to ACIM's *readings and workbook lessons*. Both enable us to focus and open the mind, so that we easily come into what yoga calls witness consciousness.

2. *Witness consciousness* in yoga is the same as *ACIM's connecting with Holy Spirit.* In witness consciousness, we become aware of that observer behind the chaos of the mind, which is an aspect of our higher self or Holy Spirit.
3. *Becoming present* is the same as ACIM's *holy instant.*
4. The *mind quiets* for both yoga and ACIM as we
5. *shift out of the ego* and come into what yoga calls
6. *illumined mind* and what the Course calls *Holy Spirit guiding the mind.*
7. This leads to what yoga calls *clear seeing* and what ACIM calls *Christ Vision,* seeing past the ego in ourselves and others.
8. In both yoga and ACIM with this clear seeing and Christ Vision, we now can *see past the illusion* (the illusion that the ego creates, in which our reality and identity are tied into the impermanent) *to the truth* (our true reality is our true nature as Spirit, whole, perfect, and eternal, where nothing can truly hurt us and we cannot truly hurt another). This is also called the *miracle* in ACIM.
9. Now there is *no more projection* in yoga and ACIM; we see ourselves clearly, so there are no more insecurities and fears to project onto others.
10. Now we are in the *experience of our true nature as pure awareness or Spirit*—from which we can live awake according to yoga or live the happy dream according to ACIM.

The Course says, "Forget not that the motivation for this course is the attainment and the keeping of the state of peace. Given this state the mind is quiet, and the condition in which God is remembered is attained." (ACIM T-24.Intro.1:1-2)

A passage in the *Bhagavad Gita* says, "The Blessed Lord said: Those who love and revere me with unwavering faith, always centering their minds on me—they are the most perfect in yoga." —*Bhagavad Gita* (Mitchell 2000, 144)

Yoga and ACIM reveal the same ultimate goal: to get quiet, to get still, so that the voice for God, Holy Spirit, can shine through. This is where we are reminded of the truth of our Oneness, with each other and with God Himself. What could be more heavenly?!

We will continue to understand in even more detail the *how-to of awakening* through the six steps we will discuss throughout this book. These will enable us to move through this 10-step *process of awakening* more easily. In the next chapter we will learn more about the illusion we experience through the ego and how it affects us in life.

CHAPTER 9

The Illusion and Its Effects

There is no life outside of Heaven. Where God created life, there life must be. In any state apart from Heaven life is illusion. At best it seems like life; at worst, like death.
                                                —ACIM T-23.II.19:1–4

Dream Analogy

ACIM and yoga liken seeing the world through the lens of the ego to an illusion or a dream, because we are not necessarily seeing what is right in front of us. We are seeing everything through the lens of the ego, through the lens of past associations and meanings that we are placing on what is now in front of us. For instance, when you give a baby a rattle, the baby stares at it. The baby puts it in his mouth and sticks his tongue all over it. The baby shakes it. The baby is in the experience of the rattle. If you gave me a rattle, I would look at it briefly and say, "Oh, that's a rattle." But I probably wouldn't consciously notice what it felt like, what color it was, what it sounded like. I immediately recognize it as a rattle, something I learned in my past, and move on.

When I run into an old acquaintance, Susie, from high school, I may talk to her for a little while and catch up. The whole time, if all I'm thinking about is how big a jerk she was in high school, then I'm seeing her through the lens of the past. The miracle and clear seeing would allow me to see Susie as a peaceful, loving Spirit, no matter how she acted back then and no matter how she might act today, whether she's still a jerk or the nicest person in the world.

When we are constantly in our heads, judging and comparing and whatever else the ego likes to do, we are living in a made-up world in our minds. It's like living in a dream. We are still in the experience of life, but we no longer notice because we are too distracted with the thoughts, judgments, and resistances that build and sustain our false ego-self. We are holding everything and everyone to the past. Even if Susie does act like a jerk today, she is acting out from something that happened in her past, rather than living in the present. If we only focus on what we are seeing through the ego lens, we get immersed in this dreamlike world and end up in all kinds of suffering. So what do we do? Let's take a look at the dream analogy.

When we see a child dreaming, and her dream turns into a nightmare, we may see her starting to thrash about or cry out. We don't then go to sleep to try to get into her dream, to fight off her monsters and bullies. We place our hand on her shoulder, gently start to rock her, and say, "It's okay baby, wake up." With ego controlling our minds, it is like we are living in a dream. We are dreaming we are separate from God and each other. Sometimes the dream is good, and sometimes it is a nightmare, but the fear of the dream becoming a nightmare is with us constantly.

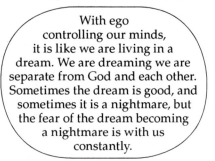

With ego controlling our minds, it is like we are living in a dream. We are dreaming we are separate from God and each other. Sometimes the dream is good, and sometimes it is a nightmare, but the fear of the dream becoming a nightmare is with us constantly.

We have to quit trying to fix the dream, which is fixing on the level of the ego. This would be equivalent to trying to get into our child's dream to fight off her monsters and bullies. It would be like coming up with something great to say to stand up for ourselves if Susie acts like a jerk to us today, like she did back in high school. *Instead*, we go through the process of getting present, getting quiet, and asking and allowing Holy Spirit to wake us up gently.

Now we can take a deep breath and begin seeing Susie in her true nature as a loving, peaceful Spirit, no matter how she acted then and no matter how she's acting now. We begin to see the connection between ourselves

On some level, Susie is picking up on your decision to see her not as separate from you but as a part of you. This affects her—and you as well—on levels we cannot even begin to fathom.

and Susie, and in doing so, we begin to draw forth our light and hers. On some level, Susie is picking up on your decision to see her not as separate from you but as a part of you. This affects her—and you as well—on levels we cannot even begin to fathom. Any ego emotion that may have come up if you had not decided to see the miracle here is totally dissipated, and you remain in a state of peace and love. What a difference!

This process of awakening is a whole lot easier to do once you've undone some of the ego. The ego is all about separation, building walls and defending those walls. Once you have undone enough of the ego, there is not much left to defend. This makes it a lot easier to remember your true nature and see the miracle here.

Understanding how the ego works and observing it in yourself and others *non-judgmentally* is key. Even once you've undone layers of ego, it can still crop up in the most unlikely of moments, sending you into a tailspin of emotion, attack, and defense. Don't fret! This is simply another opportunity for you to remember what you've learned about your ego-self and allow more compassion to fill your heart for yourself and others, as we all deal with this same beast. Yoga practice helps undo layer by layer of this ego cloud, but most importantly, it teaches us to simply be observant with absolutely no judgment.

Why Doesn't God Just Awaken Us Himself?

I once asked my Dad: If God is all-powerful and all-knowing, why doesn't He wake us up Himself? If He knows some of us are having such bad experiences with the ego, why doesn't He just wake us up? If you believe that God dwells within us, then why doesn't that aspect of ourselves wake us up or clue us in?

My dad helped me understand this. God doesn't wake us up automatically, because He loves us unconditionally and with unconditional love comes total freedom. God knows we are only dreaming, that it is simply imaginary lines and walls keeping us from seeing our connection with Him and each other, and that all the pain and suffering we seem to be experiencing in this world is not our true reality. Deep down, we know we chose to experience this ego thought system, and God is allowing us to do so. In other words, we have the freedom to experience this ego-self and it's thought and belief system for as long as we want.

However, God also knows that we are stuck in this made-up ego mental construct. He knows we are stuck in the dream, thinking these imaginary lines and walls are real and impenetrable. God doesn't want us to suffer, not even for one minute, even though He knows we are not truly suffering. In actuality, God *is* gently trying to awaken us in every moment through the Holy Spirit, through our higher self.

But because of this total freedom, we have to get to a point where *we* choose to tune in and listen to Holy Spirit's guidance. God and the Holy Spirit will not force it on us. ACIM calls it a "little willingness." We have to have this little willingness to decide we have had enough of this ego experience and want to wake up. As soon as you decide this, as soon as you have that "little willingness," guess what?

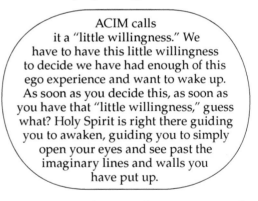

ACIM calls it a "little willingness." We have to have this little willingness to decide we have had enough of this ego experience and want to wake up. As soon as you decide this, as soon as you have that "little willingness," guess what? Holy Spirit is right there guiding you to awaken, guiding you to simply open your eyes and see past the imaginary lines and walls you have put up.

Holy Spirit is right there guiding you to awaken, guiding you to simply open your eyes and see past the imaginary lines and walls you have put up. You are guided to read a book like Choose Spirit Now. You are guided to be able to see the miracle, rather than going into the habitual patterns of seeing through the lens of the ego.

Some of these concepts are difficult to grasp, but this is where that gentle awakening comes in. Holy Spirit, your higher self, knows when you are ready to understand the next step, the next concept, and won't help you to understand the next step until you are ready. You simply have to choose to be open to your higher self's guidance and trust it to lead you gently out of the false ego-self that we have all been so immersed in for so long.

> Holy Spirit, your higher self, knows when you are ready to understand the next step, the next concept, and won't help you to understand the next step until you are ready. You simply have to choose to be open to your higher self's guidance and trust it to lead you gently out of the false ego-self that we have all been so immersed in for so long.

The Illusion—ACIM

Let's look at this dreamlike world, this illusion according to ACIM, more closely. In the introduction to the Course, it says this: "The course does not aim at teaching the meaning of love, for that is beyond what can be taught. It does aim, however, at removing the blocks to the awareness of love's presence, which is your natural inheritance. The opposite of love is fear, but what is all-encompassing can have no opposite" (ACIM In.1:6–8).

Here, ACIM says that the Course is aiming to remove the blocks to the awareness of love's presence. Those blocks are the ego cloud we've been talking about. So what does this mean? If ego cannot really exist as love's opposite because love is all-encompassing, then how can it block love's presence?

It is like an optical illusion. We have developed this ego-self based on past experiences. The ego is simply a collection of thoughts, beliefs, judgments, and attachments based on the past, and all the emotions that stem from those thoughts, beliefs, etc. This creates the illusion of a cloud surrounding us. We see everything through this ego cloud, so we are not seeing clearly.

When we judge and resist life, it simply serves to make the ego cloud *seem* more real, more dense, and opaque. However, when you look at this ego cloud head on and shine the light on it, you then experience it fully, and it burns up and disappears. When we begin establishing witness consciousness and are able to poke our heads out of the ego cloud and see that we are immersed in it, we can now study it. By studying it and observing it non-judgmentally, we actually cause it to disappear or be undone. The ego's thoughts, beliefs, judgments, attachments, and all the subsequent emotions these cause are like a figment of our imagination.

When we decide to turn the light of self-study onto them, they eventually disappear and uncloud our vision of Oneness.

ACIM says: "There is no life outside of Heaven. Where God created life, there life must be. In any state apart from Heaven life is illusion. At best it seems like life; at worst, like death" (ACIM T-23.II.19:1–4).

God created us in perfection. As we utilize the practice to understand and experience our true nature, we begin to see clearly beyond the illusion and experience the happy dream. We are in full realization that we are One with each other and with God; nothing that is happening on the level of form or of the ego can take that truth from us. *This does not mean life is perfect;* it means we understand that this imperfection is part of the ego illusion and has absolutely no effect on our true nature in Spirit. This keeps us in a state of peace throughout whatever hardships or imperfections we come across in life. In other words, we are still aware of and awake to our true nature, even among the illusion of the ego.

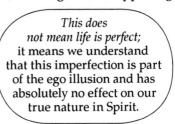

This does not mean life is perfect; it means we understand that this imperfection is part of the ego illusion and has absolutely no effect on our true nature in Spirit.

When we are not experiencing this happy dream, we are identifying with the ego, with the illusion. This illusion can be pleasant or even wonderful, or it can be a downright nightmare. Either way, it is an illusion and can be awakened from. The ones who are having a wonderful experience in the illusion still benefit from awakening. When you are misidentifying yourself with the ego-self, a wonderful illusion of a life can turn into a nightmare at a moment's notice. When you are living life awake, you rest peacefully no matter what may come up throughout life, good or bad.

When you are living life awake, you rest peacefully no matter what may come up throughout life, good or bad.

The Illusion—Yoga

Let's look at the illusion according to yoga. The following is a Sanskrit mantra from one of the *upanishads*, which is an ancient eastern philosophical text.

> *"asato mā sad gamaya tamaso mā jyotir gamaya mrityor mā amritam gamaya om shanti, shanti, shanti"*
> —Sanskrit mantra from the *Bryhadaranyaka Upanisad* 1.3.28 (Wikipedia 2014)

It means: "Lead us from the unreal to the real, lead us from darkness to light, lead us from death to immortality, let there be peace, peace, peace." This can also be seen as: Lead us from ego to spirit, lead us from ego to spirit, lead us from ego to spirit, let there be peace eternal, which is the experience of spirit.

Let's break it down. "Lead us from the unreal to the real" (*Brihadaranyaka Upanishad* 1.3.28). The unreal is the illusion, which is the ego's view that our reality is the body, impermanent and seemingly separate. The unreal is the illusion, the cloud of old thoughts, beliefs, and judgments that we transpose onto what is in front of us now. The real is the bliss or the happy dream in which we remember our true nature as Spirit and remember our true reality as whole, perfect, and eternal. We then can stay in peace even amid the hardships in this life, because we know they are having no real effect on our true nature as Spirit.

"Lead us from darkness to light" (*Brihadaranyaka Upanishad* 1.3.28). The darkness is all the negativity symbolic of the ego thought system controlling the mind, obscuring our light of Spirit. The darkness is the ego cloud surrounding us, blocking us from being able to see the connection between our light and the light of all of creation. The light is the Spirit, unconditional love filled with peace, joy, and happiness, in which we were created in God's image. The light is the connection between us all, every aspect of creation, that extends to infinity for eternity, leaving nothing and no one outside of it. The light represents the unconditional love, deep peace, and abundant joy that constitutes our true nature. The light shines through the illusion of the ego cloud, causing it to disappear like the optical illusion that it is.

"Lead us from death to immortality" (*Brihadaranyaka Upanishad* 1.3.28). Death is the ultimate fear in the ego's thought system because of the mistaken belief that the body and made-up ego self-image is our reality. Immortality is our right as eternal Spirit created by God in His image.

> Immortality is our right as eternal Spirit created by God in His image.

This *upanishad* is a prayer to our highest self to lead us to clear out the imaginary ego cloud that surrounds us and lead us to the truth of who we really are as whole, perfect, and eternal. The *upanishads* are thousands of years old, and it is fascinating that this idea to wake up out of the unreal has been around for so long.

The Effect of Staying in the Illusion

Let's look at the effect of simply staying in the illusion and continuing on the way most of us have been.

When we look out on the world or in our own lives through our ego filter and we see problems that make us sad, scared, angry, etc., these emotions don't do anything for the world. They just block our light, peace, love, and higher guidance, which causes more suffering in us. In other words, it *extends* the suffering. It may feel like we are doing something worthwhile by staying in these potent emotions, but if we are doing something in a state of anger, sadness, pity, blame, or fear, then we are still suffering. How can we create a world of peace and love from a state of suffering? We can't. When we go into these potent emotions, we usually then react with ego-driven solutions, or we end up in a wellspring of guilt

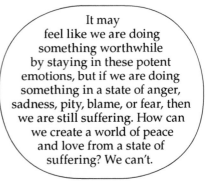

for not being able to find a solution at all. We must learn to express these emotions properly and let them go, rather than allow them to draw us further into the ego mind-set. In a later chapter we will learn how the yoga practice helps us to express these emotions and let them go completely, taking us out of suffering. Eventually, we learn to bypass these emotions altogether as we learn to awaken completely.

In the next chapter we will understand more in depth the happy dream we experience through living from Spirit and how positive its effect is on us in life.

CHAPTER 10

The Happy Dream and Its Effects & Step 2 to Awakening

We can change ourselves and we can change the world simultaneously.
—Amit Goswami, PhD, *The Quantum Activist* DVD (2009)

The Happy Dream

When we tune in and allow Holy Spirit to guide us to see past the illusion of the ego, then we can live this human experience in full realization of the truth of our Oneness and live what ACIM calls the happy dream. We are living in the holy instant, experiencing the miracle of seeing ourselves and others in our true nature as one with each other, one with Holy Spirit, and one with God.

This doesn't mean life is perfect. It means we remember ourselves in our true nature among life experiences and can enjoy even the seemingly "bad" experiences, because we know they have no real effect on our true nature. We begin to notice that our perception (of things that are happening in our lives) is changing and keeping us on more of an even keel.

Toward the end of my teacher training at Kripalu, we did an experiment where we broke up into groups of five and sat in a circle. We each took a turn getting into the middle of the circle, while the other four held a sacred space with intent. The person in the middle was supposed to close his or her eyes and go into a spontaneous yoga flow, a movement meditation that is the hallmark of Kripalu yoga.

At this point in our training, we were all doing yoga for the better part of the day, twelve days in a row. We knew stuff about each other, deep personal stuff that some of us had not even told close friends or family members before. We had trust in each other and love for each other, even though we knew we would be together for just a short while.

When it was my turn to be in the middle, I had an experience of really "seeing" my connection to God. I saw (in my mind's eye) gold flecks raining down, over and through all of us. The gold flecks were love and grace; they were God. I felt in that moment unquestionably connected to God and everything else. I had had moments of feeling this unquestionable connection before, but this was the first time I could *see* the connection through this gold-flecked rain. I knew at that moment I would never have to question that connection again.

It was powerful enough to wipe out any uncertainty, doubt, or loneliness that crept up on me in any moment after that. It was like getting my foot in the door on this enlightenment thing. Now all I had to do was stay on the path and remember that there is no door, there is no wall, there is no cloud.

Yoga in its Purest Form

The meaning of yoga as "union" became very simple to me. I had been overwhelmed at times by the different styles and schools of yoga, but I finally got it. In its purest form, yoga is about seeing through the ego and resting in our truest nature as pure awareness, which is Spirit, as often as possible. I could let go of the ego's need to learn it all, because now I understood what yoga was truly all about. Yoga can be anything that takes us out of the ego's habitual way of thinking, analyzing, and separating

> The meaning of yoga as "union" became very simple to me. I had been overwhelmed at times by the different styles and schools of yoga, but I finally got it. In its purest form, yoga is about seeing through the ego and resting in our truest nature as pure awareness, which is Spirit, as often as possible.

79

and reminds us of this union, our Oneness with all of creation, and with God Himself.

The Ego's "Problem" with a Peace-Filled Life

Living life in peace does not jibe with the ego. As a matter of fact, this seems cruel from an ego standpoint, because emotion, according to the ego, makes the world meaningful. The ego thrives on emotion; it is the lifeblood.

Your ego-self is going to convince you that you would rather choose a life of emotion, of "meaning," rather than this emotionless, meaningless world of Spirit. The ego-self sees its emotional world as meaningful and the nonemotional world of Spirit as meaningless. The only emotions that belong to Spirit are peace and joy, because these are attributes of unconditional love in which we were created. They are different than the ego emotions we are used to. The ego makes us think that true caring is getting sad, angry, fearful, etc., but in reality, if we really wake up and look, those emotions only cause more suffering if we don't know how to release them. Here's the kicker: If we learn how to release these emotions with Spirit's help and guidance, we can actually enjoy these ego emotions as we experience and release them through the light of Spirit.

Spirit's Peace-Filled Life (the Happy Dream) as the Most Meaningful Way to Live

The ego will try to convince us that living from Spirit sounds meaningless and careless. Living from Spirit is *not* meaningless or careless! When you see *everything* as connected, as One, then

80

everything does matter and you do care, because everything is a part of the whole.

It's simply a different way of caring than what the ego is used to. It's a different way of looking at "it does matter" than what the ego is used to. The ego thinks that for something to matter, it must attach some dramatic, passionate emotion to it, but that just isn't so.

> The ego thinks that for something to matter, it must attach some dramatic, passionate emotion to it, but that just isn't so.

This does not mean we sit idly by while bad things happen and we're okay with it. We stay in that peaceful state of believing that nothing can truly affect our true nature as perfection. If I can look at suffering in the world and remember that underneath all the form is perfect Spirit, all one, all connected, then I can let that peace, light, and love shine forth from my true nature. That does more for the world than anything else. Staying in the peaceful state of Spirit does more for the world than getting sad, fearful, or angry, which can lead to blame, judgment, and depression, which is *more* suffering. By staying in that peaceful place, we can actually draw forth positive change into the world beyond our human mind's ability to fathom. But this positive change has to come from a place of peace and guidance, not from a place of suffering as we wallow in unexpressed emotion.

> If you have a choice, *which we do,* why not choose to live from this peaceful state of Spirit, especially when you realize that it has the most powerful, positive impact on the level of the world?

If you have a choice, *which we do,* why not choose to live from this peaceful state of Spirit, especially when you realize that it has the most powerful, positive impact on the level of the world? Because the ego has tricked us into thinking that what is up is down, and we get so totally turned around, we cannot see straight.

The reality is, we *can* make this life the most

> The reality is, we *can* make this life the most wonderful experience possible by seeing through the ego and living the happy dream. Again, it doesn't mean life is perfect, but it *does mean* that our lives and the lives around us are changing for the better by us simply staying connected to and guided from this peaceful state of Spirit as much as possible, and channeling that peace into the world from within.

wonderful experience possible by seeing through the ego and living the happy dream. Again, it doesn't mean life is perfect, but it *does mean* that our lives and the lives around us are changing for the better by us simply staying connected to and guided from this peaceful state of Spirit as much as possible, and channeling that peace into the world from within.

Some of us are guided to simply be still in peace. Think of the cloistered nuns, monks, and others who are in constant prayer and meditation. That is having a most positive and transformational effect on the level of the world.

My Own Ego Drama

My marital relationship in my twenties was indicative of my mind-set, that the more drama in a relationship, the more meaningful it must be. Granted, my ex at times gave me fuel for the fire, but I fed on the need for drama. It was a deeply engrained behavior I had learned in childhood. It brought me back to that old, familiar feeling of "poor me." Crazy jealousy reared its ugly head countless times in the beginning of the marriage, and crazy behavior soon followed.

When I began practicing yoga consistently, I began to see things differently, and I was able to let go of some of my jealousy and insecurity. My yoga practice enabled me to break that pattern of drama. I finally realized that needing drama in a relationship was completely backward! Unconditional love has no drama. It is total freedom, total peace, total joy.

The more I practiced yoga and re-connected with this peace inside the more I was able to let go of that "poor me" feeling that I had been attached to for so long. I was able to shift out of all the dramatic ego emotions, which enabled me to tune into my higher guidance and the clear knowledge that ending this relationship would be the best thing for me. Now I was able to let the relationship end peacefully, rather than cling on and allow my ego to drag us through more drama and strife. Granted it wasn't always easy, but deep down I knew that this decision *felt* right.

More Positive Effects of Living the Happy Dream

Amit Goswami, PhD is professor emeritus of theoretical quantum physics from the University of Oregon, where he taught since 1968. He now teaches at the Holmes Institute for Philosophical Research in Los Angeles, and his textbook, *Quantum Mechanics,* serves as the standard intro in many universities as the essential mathematics of quantum physics.

Dr. Goswami says in the film, *The Quantum Activist,* "We have to get into an altered state of consciousness. Then we can do a lot with our intention, and there is experimental data proving that" (Goswami 2009).

You may have noticed that in the beginning of yoga class, there is usually an intention set for the practice. It is always something for the good of the whole. People do it when they pray and then come into meditation. Coming into a meditative state after setting an intention actually puts that intention into a more active, creative state, eventually making the intention a reality.

Dr. Goswami says, "Intentions do work. Ordinary ego intentions don't work because we never go beyond the ego. But if we can somehow manifest collective consciousness, manifest nonlocal consciousness; make our intentions on the basis of nonlocal consciousness; if our individual intention resonates with nonlocal consciousness by some means or other, then intentions can come true" (Goswami 2009).

When you talk to people who have been doing yoga consistently for a number of years, and you ask them what the practice has done for them, what you will hear repeatedly is, "Yoga has changed my life." Across the board, you will hear how yoga, over time, transformed people's lives for the better. And it does. Yoga enables us to quiet the ego controlling the mind, tune in to our inner guidance, and follow that guidance that leads to big, positive changes in our lives.

The best part about yoga is, these changes that it brings about come from the inside out, not a forced outside-in change, so the transformation is almost unnoticed. You simply look around one day and realize how far you've come from several years ago or whenever it was you first started your practice.

Dr. Goswami also says in *The Quantum Activist:*

> In those moments, lucid moments when we are walking on the beach, when we are walking in the woods, in those very blissful moments we do go into our pre-conscious. We don't sift our experience through the memories and it is then a wonderful, lucid experience of that present moment, just that moment. This is the moment that is called the moment of *satori* in Japanese, a moment of *samadhi* in Hinduism. This is the moment when Christians say that "I became the Holy Spirit" or "Holy Spirit was speaking through me." These are moments of cosmic awareness. We become aware that I am not an isolated individual. I am the whole world. (Goswami 2009)

Wow! Here is a quantum physicist saying that when we go into these lucid moments, we have an experience of realizing that we are not separate but that we are connected with all of creation. The same thing the yogis have been saying for thousands of years! Through more and more experiences of these altered states in which we access pure awareness of Spirit, we begin to live the happy dream in which there is no more separation, isolation, and loneliness indicative of the ego mind-set. There is only an understanding of Oneness, inclusion, and pure joy. As we live the happy dream, we are in total communication with our higher self, with Holy Spirit. We are now guided through life effortlessly, through our inner guidance, through our intuition. We tap into unlimited creativity and connection as we are "inspired." We live in perfect harmony with all of creation, knowing that we are all one. We now feel perfectly fulfilled, happy, joyful, and peaceful, and we extend unconditional love to everyone we meet.

The Happy Dream and Bliss as Ordinary Moments

Where some of us may get confused is in expecting extraordinary moments every time we experience living awake through yoga and the happy dream.

The reality is that the happy dream and living awake is simply ourselves immersed in the experience of whatever is

> Many make the mistake that living awake should feel really different. The truth is, life does seem richer, but you still feel normal. You may have more moments in tears of joy at the gratitude you feel for life and its experience as you are fully immersed in it.

happening at that moment. It's not some fireworks-exploding event. It is a very contented, peaceful and joyful state, but not in the way the ego might expect. Many make the mistake that living awake should feel really different. The truth is, life does seem richer, but you still feel normal. You may have more moments in tears of joy at the gratitude you feel for life and its experience as you are fully immersed in it.

Step 2 to Awakening

In step 2 to awakening, we learn to discern between ego and spirit. We learn to discern between living in the illusion or the happy dream. When we are living the happy dream, we see our truest nature as beyond the body and the mind, even within the experience of the body and the mind. Here, Spirit can guide the mind, and we feel calm and peaceful. The mind is quiet. Whenever you feel peaceful and calm, you can rest assured that you are living from Spirit.

When we are living in the illusion, we are associating and limiting our truest nature with the body and the mind. Ego is distracting and controlling the mind with thoughts, old beliefs, and judgments, so we feel fearful, worried, anxious, and stressed. There is a storm in the mind. Whenever you feel anxious or stressed, you can be sure that you are living from ego.

Step 2 to awakening is simply to notice how you feel and let that be a signal as to whether you are living in the illusion or the happy dream. When you are feeling anxious, worried, and stressed, you are living in the ego-self. You believe you are separate from everyone else, that you can hurt and be hurt. When you feel calm, peaceful, and relaxed, you are living in Spirit, remembering your true nature as one, and connected with everyone else.

> When you are feeling anxious, worried, and stressed, you are living in the ego-self. You believe you are separate from everyone else, that you can hurt and be hurt. When you feel calm, peaceful, and relaxed, you are living in Spirit, remembering your true nature as one, and connected with everyone else.

Remember, it's about discernment, not judgment. There is a big difference! When you find yourself judging, take a deep breath, smile, and let that judgment go. It's about simply discerning where you are living from, and that's it. No need to go a step further and make a judgment about it. This only brings the ego into it even more.

For most of us, we will be moving back and forth between living from ego and living from spirit, and that's okay. In the next several chapters, we will learn how yoga helps us to undo the ego, layer by layer, by working with what comes up as we are still immersed in this ego mind-set. This helps us immensely in our ability to shed more and more of this ego cloud so that we can live awake in more and more moments.

CHAPTER 11

Self-Taught Yoga Practice

Truly, the wise proclaim that love is the only path, love is the
only God, and love is the only scripture.
—Swami Kripalu (Levitt 2004, 119)

Self-Taught Yoga

What first caught my attention about hatha yoga was that I could not do
it. My first yoga class ever was in massage school. All I can remember
was getting into plow pose and realizing, A, that I couldn't do it, and B,
that I was going to do it anyway, because I should be able to do anything
at age twenty-two. My first class, and I was already learning how much
I push myself, no matter what the cost: headache!

At twenty-four, I bought my first yoga video with Nadia Jenkins, a local
yoga teacher. I was fairly athletic and in good shape, so when I couldn't
do triangle pose without falling, my interest was piqued. I had always
loved a physical challenge, and so began my hatha yoga practice.

After my divorce at twenty-eight, I kept the house, a 1926 bungalow, and
made one of the bedrooms into a yoga room. I had a mirror installed on
one wall, painted the walls a beautiful teal green, and set up an altar
with a Buddha statue and other meaningful things.

I had been doing yoga fairly consistently at this point for about three
years, but after my divorce, my practice really began. I added poses
I would see in *Yoga Journal* to *vinyasa* flows I had learned in my yoga
video. I didn't realize it at the time, but self-teaching allowed me to

learn yoga as meditation in motion and follow what my intuition was guiding me to do, rather than follow a particular script.

In the privacy of my new yoga room, I was surprised to find myself sobbing through particular poses. I had all sorts of emotions coming up and out: anger, sadness, frustration, irritation, and feelings of achingly painful loneliness. But as I stayed in certain poses and kept breathing, the sobbing eventually stopped, and I felt an immense peacefulness surrounding me. I felt my intuition becoming second nature. I felt like I was releasing all those pent-up emotions from childhood, emotions that I never could completely express or work through in any sort of intellectual manner before now.

I was also working through living alone after my four-year marriage and the worry that I would never find the right person for me. This sobbing through my yoga practice went on for about two years. Even with all the tears, I realized I was feeling more and more settled with myself, comfortable with who I was. It was a difficult time, in that I was going through a lot of new emotions, but now I had this beautiful practice that was helping me to let them go.

I was experiencing firsthand what yoga could really do. I didn't want to get sucked back into a depression and lose this practice that I felt was helping me so immensely. I wanted to solidify it more into my life, and I decided that going to yoga-teacher training might help me do this. I had no desire to be a teacher, but I wanted to learn as much as possible about the yogic philosophy. My cousin and his wife, who lived in New Jersey at the time, had mentioned to me that I would love to visit Kripalu, a former ashram, now a yoga center in the beautiful Berkshire Hills of western Massachusetts.

Kripalu

In 2006, I went to Kripalu and had another transformative, life-altering experience. Since teacher training involves doing yoga anywhere from five to ten or more hours a day, it can get pretty intense. Talk about being present!

I fell in love with my teachers, Megha and Devarshi, who had both actually lived at Kripalu when it was an ashram. The stories they told us of Swami Kripalu, the guru whom Kripalu is named after, and of life at the ashram were beautiful and interesting. I learned that Swami Kripalu met his own teacher the day he planned on taking his own life, something I could definitely relate to after my bouts with depression.

There was a small chapel area in which Swami Kripalu's things were set up, including his altar, his books, his robe, and his slippers. The first time I went in there to meditate I realized that as soon as I entered this curtained-off space, my mind got quiet, and I experienced peace and stillness without having to do a thing. Simply sitting among the Swami's personal effects brought me into this space of resounding peace that was so deep, it was mesmerizing.

They say Swami Kripalu was doing more than ten hours of yoga/ meditation a day in the form of breath work, movement, and hand *mudras*. I could understand how he was in such a peaceful place; simply sitting among his things allowed me to pick up on that stillness and that peace.

Kripalu said:

> Truly, the wise proclaim that love is the only path, love is the only God, and love is the only scripture. Love brings union by healing the split between the body, mind, and heart. United, they merge with the soul just as countless rivers and streams merge into the vast ocean. Without love, light cannot be kindled in our hearts, our homes, or in the world. Love is the only worldwide religion. Whether you're reading the scriptures of the Vedas, the Koran, or the Bible, they're meaningless without love. Love is my only path. In fact, I'm a pilgrim on the path of love. (Levitt 2004, 119–120)

Atma Jo Ann Levitt compiled and edited a book called *Pilgrim of Love: The Life and Teachings of Swami Kripalu*, if you'd like to read more about this extraordinary man. The beauty in his words moved me, and I knew that I had found a piece of my path in Kripalu's yoga.

What I had come to Kripalu for is exactly what I received: a renewed dedication to the practice. My life had changed miraculously since I had

89

begun this practice. Peace and contentment now outweighed the blues and depression, and this was what enabled me to make yoga my first priority, before my job that I loved or my social life that was dwindling. I realized toward the end of my training that I did want to teach this beautiful, ancient practice. How could I not want to share what had become the most important thing in my life? What felt like a life's purpose and a final purpose to my practice was only the beginning of what my practice would lead me to: the only goal that matters—living life awake!

CHAPTER 12

Yoga: Undoing the Ego

If you are not in charge of your attention, you are not in charge of your choice. It's the key of yoga.
—Devarshi Steven Hartman, *The Essence of the Bhagavad Gita* CD collection (Hartman 2013)

Why Is It Important to Understand What Yoga Is Doing for Us?

Whether we know what yoga is doing for us or not, it will still have the same positive effect. But taking the time to understand what yoga is doing shortens the path to undoing the ego and living awake in more and more moments.

Imagine if you could know the effect your smile might have on someone else's day. When we walk down the street and decide to look up and smile at someone, we may never know the effect of that smile on that person's day. But imagine if I sat you down and said, "I'm going to show you a video of how your smile affected that person and their day, and how they then looked up and smiled at someone else, and how that smile then affected that person's day," and so on. If you could see the effect of that smile and how many people it affected positively, you would probably be more apt to look up and smile at people more often.

It is the same with yoga practices. If you understand the positive effect of the practice on you, your loved ones, and the world around you, then you will probably be more apt to practice.

My Suffering

In my early twenties, I was still carrying around a lot of anger and resentment from the childhood drama, and I didn't know how to let it go. About once a year, some poor soul would come around and say or do the wrong thing, and I would blow up at them, letting them have it. I was bottling so much up that every now and then, I needed to release some of that energy. I ruined several relationships in my life at that time by doing this, unhealthy for me and for the other person.

But at twenty-two, I came across a book by Dr. Christiane Northrup called *Women's Bodies, Women's Wisdom*. I'm going to share a quote from this book that I actually wrote down at the time on an index card and carried around with me for a long time. This is what Dr. Northrup says: "Anger is energy—our personal jet fuel. It is telling us that something needs adjustment in our lives. It is telling us that there is something we want that we don't know we want." She goes on to say, "This emotion is dangerous only if we deny it and stuff it in our bodies. Anger and all other 'negative' emotions can serve us well when we don't turn them in on ourselves as depression or lash out with them against others" (Northrup 2002, 604).

These negative emotions are signals, and what they are telling us is that we are stuck again in the ego's thought system and belief system. We feel totally cut off from our higher self and are probably making choices based on the ego rather than our higher self's guidance. This can leave us frustrated and angry without realizing why. When Dr. Northrup says anger is telling us that "there is something that we want that we don't know we want," this is where that search for our true home comes in. We are searching far and wide for all sorts of things, but what underlies it all is the desire to come back home to our true nature in which we are open to and in tune with our higher guidance, making life a more peaceful, wonderful experience.

Yoga can help. First, it can help by allowing us to face our anger and all the other negative emotions that we anticipate to be too painful to face. Once we do, we can then release them which enables us to let go in to our true nature more easily, a much more peaceful and joyful state to be in. Now we will be tuned into our higher guidance once again, guiding us to get back on a track that feels good and feels right. It took me two more years from first reading this passage from Dr. Northrup to begin my yoga practice. But once I did, I felt the anger that was always bottled up just beneath the surface begin to dissipate. What a blessing. It was many years later that I would understand how yoga was getting me back to a life that felt worth living, a life filled with peace and contentment, rather than anger and strife.

Yoga as a Practice

Yoga practices work on two levels:

1. Yoga works to thin out the ego cloud layer by layer.
2. Yoga works to help you rise above the ego cloud altogether.

I frequently lead an ego-release meditation that really helps us to understand how the ego mind works. When we imagine the Oneness of all of creation as light, extending to infinity, there is nowhere that this light does not exist. But among the light is manifested form, so you can see our different bodies and forms within the light. Surrounding each of our bodies are clouds. Some clouds are light and wispy, so that part of the light still shines through, and some clouds are dense and dark, obscuring the light completely. The clouds represent the ego. The clouds in no way affect the light extending to infinity, but they do seem to obscure and separate the light. Some people are surrounded by dense, dark clouds and some by light, wispy clouds. The effect that the ego has on these people is in direct relation to how dense and dark the cloud surrounding them is. ACIM says, "The light is in you. Darkness can cover it, but cannot put it out." (ACIM T-18.III.1:7-8)

Yoga, on an initial level, begins to actually thin out the ego clouds, so that we begin to see through the clouds to our connection with all of creation as this light. This is really helpful to anyone who may be so immersed in the ego that they are seeing little or no light at all. *But yoga also enables us to poke our heads above the clouds and see that in reality, they don't do a thing to break our connection with the light of all creation.* They only seem to block this connection from time to time depending on how dense and dark they come to be. This is great because as we continue to study the ego we realize that we can be fully immersed in this ego cloud but totally unaffected by it as we stay in a higher state of consciousness as we observe it.

How One Level Leads to the Next

There seem to be levels to awakening, layers of ego mind that we have to let go of one by one. Yoga works to actually let go of these layers of ego mind, to thin out these ego clouds obscuring the light. Eventually we have thinned out enough of these clouds to be able to see that they aren't real to begin with. Initially it feels as if we are poking our heads above the clouds to see our connection in light. But eventually we are able to "see" in a way in which all the clouds disappear altogether. This is called "clear seeing" in yoga and "the miracle" (Christ Vision) in ACIM.

Witness Consciousness: Key to Yoga

When we focus our attention, we come into witness consciousness, a very peaceful place where we are quietly observing with no judgment. Yoga practice helps us to slow down and get quiet enough so we begin to notice witness consciousness.

As we focus our attention on the breath or on the pose, we take the mind out of its habitual way of thinking, analyzing, and judging, and we are able to notice this peaceful place inside.

We begin to notice that this peaceful place is separate from the ego thoughts and noise going on in the mind. This takes us deeper into step 2 of awakening, in which we are discerning between ego and spirit. Now we are in a state of consciousness, witness consciousness, in which we really begin to see all the thoughts and noise in our heads as something separate, rather than thinking it's the real us. We begin to realize that the calm, peaceful state we are accessing from within is actually a quality of our true nature to which we are awakening. Witness consciousness is a state of mind that our higher self utilizes to wake us up. Now we are beginning to see the ego as a cloud that can

> Witness consciousness is a state of mind that our higher self utilizes to wake us up.

come and go, but not anything permanent, and definitely not our true nature.

Little by little, as this truth sinks in, we naturally begin detaching from the ego thoughts and noise. Now we are fully in charge of our attention, and from here, we can choose which state we want to live from—the peaceful state or the one with all the thoughts and noise going on. We can choose to stay immersed in the cloud or poke our heads out and send it on its way. If you didn't believe it before, now you can see and understand how you can become immersed in this ego thought system without even realizing it. But now you also can see and understand that there is a way out. As my teacher, Devarshi says, "If you are not in charge of your attention, you are not in charge of your choice. It's the key of yoga." (Hartman 2013) This ability to begin focusing the mind in witness consciousness is the key of yoga and what allows us to begin waking up from ego consciousness (the ego's thought system) as we lift ourselves out of this ego cloud.

When I was taking my teacher-training course at Kripalu, we spent a good bit of time discerning witness consciousness from the fleeting thoughts with which we think of ourselves. I was really able to see the difference for the first time between my ego (the steady stream of thoughts, which seemed like me, running through my head all the time) and witness consciousness (the quiet, still, peaceful, and non-judgmentally witnessing aspect of myself). The more we practice coming into witness consciousness, the easier it becomes, until we soon find ourselves living from this observant, peaceful state automatically. This in't full awakening since we are still in consciousness, but it's a great place to live from in the meantime and an integral part of living life awake.

Most of us will not be able to live in pure awareness in every moment. We must utilize consciousness in this human experience. As we develop witness consciousness, we can now live in what yoga calls unbounded consciousness (an awakened state of consciousness) in which we are no longer bound by the ego. Living life awake means we are living from witness consciousness part of the time, always fully aware of the ego cloud as we work on thinning it out or rising out of it completely, but we are also allowing ourselves moments of full letting go of consciousness into pure awareness through meditation or any activities which take us momentarily out of consciousness.

Ego as Mental and Emotional Tension in the Body

The ego's thought system (ego consciousness) causes stress. Under the ego's thought system, we resist life with our thoughts, judgments, beliefs, and then we are subject to the subsequent emotions that stem from these thoughts, judgments, and beliefs. We can then resist the emotions, so we don't have to feel the anticipated pain they may bring with them. All of this resistance is then stored in our bodies as stress and tension.

In yoga practice, this stored stress and resistance will be felt initially as physical sensation or tension in the body. When you start this practice, at first it feels like a tight hamstring. Then, as you tune in deeper, you will notice emotion coming up behind that physical tension. Tension and stress in the body is simply an indicator of resistance going on in the mind, an indicator that we are living in ego consciousness with the ego in complete control. We have forgotten the bigger picture and we have become bogged down in the human experience. Remember, when ego is controlling the mind, we experience stress and anxiety. When Spirit is guiding the mind, we feel peaceful and calm.

Stress-anxiety = ego. Peace-calm = Spirit.

Yoga: Accessing and Undoing the Ego

Because we can trap and store stress in the body, each yoga pose has the potential to access this stored stress in a specific part of the body and ultimately release it. When we come into a particular pose and experience the initial physical sensation (tension) that may be arising, we come into witness consciousness and begin focusing our attention on these sensations. In witness consciousness, we simply observe non-judgmentally.

As we stay focused in witness consciousness, we concentrate on the physical sensations that are arising. Usually we begin to notice stored emotion rising up behind the physical sensation. There may be an intense desire to get out of the pose and a desire to hold the breath. We can tap into this emotion and allow ourselves to really experience it and release it by deepening the breath and remaining focused on all the physical, mental, and emotional sensations that are arising. Now we can "ride the wave of sensation," one of the hallmarks of Kripalu Yoga, in which we ride out the discomfort of these sensations until we come back to a state of peace.

This takes discipline and dedication. When we have that initial desire to get out of the pose, the desire to hold the breath, that's when we make a conscious effort to do the opposite. We deepen the breath. We stay in the pose. We ride that wave out and see what may come up. All kinds of emotion may arise that we didn't even know was lurking beneath the surface. We access these emotions with each *focused inhale of breath* and we release these emotions

> We access these emotions with each *focused inhale of breath* and we release these emotions through each *focused exhale of breath.*

through each *focused exhale of breath.* Sometimes these focused inhalations begin accessing more intense emotional energy and this can lead us into a good, old cry. This is great! Here we are really coming face-to-face with this deeply-held emotional stress and tension. Crying simply helps us to wring out this more deeply-held emotional energy through the more forceful exhalations that come with crying. Once these feelings are expressed and released completely, then we find ourselves reveling in an ocean of peace.

You may not ever cry through your yoga practice, but it can happen, especially if you have a lot of intense and deeply-held emotional trauma to let go of. I always recommend practicing on your own, in the privacy of your own home. In some classes, you may feel safe enough to cry if it comes to that point, and that's wonderful. Just know that it is worth practicing at home to see if that's what needs to happen. Once you have expressed these emotions fully, you realize that your body is more relaxed and your mind is quiet. You have released this negative emotional energy, this stored stress indicative of your misidentification with the ego-self and the ego's control over the mind. You have undone this particular ego cloud.

What Deep Breathing Is Really Doing as It Accesses the Emotional Center of the Body in the Lower Belly

In many traditions, the lower belly is considered the emotional center of the body. If you have ever found yourself sobbing, you may have noticed a deep muscular contraction in the belly as you exhale your sob, as if you are wringing yourself out emotionally. Within the chakra system, the second chakra is found in the lower belly. The second chakra represents the emotional body, and this is where some of our most potent, powerful emotions arise from. We can access stored memory and stress from any area of the body, but the lower belly holds the bulk of this emotional energy attached to our memories.

When you take a deep, focused breath into the lower belly, you are accessing this emotional center and the emotional energy which is stored there. When this happens, you may notice a desire to hold your breath. If you want to undo ego, it is important to keep the breath deep. You can come into the *ujjayi* breath, which is known as the purifying, cleansing breath in yoga. The *ujjayi* breath is a more focused breath and helps to release this stored emotional energy through the exhale.

The *ujjayi* breath is also called the ocean-sounding breath, because when done correctly, it is very calming and soothing, like an ocean. The mouth is closed, and there is a gentle constriction at the base of the throat as you make an audible ocean sound as you inhale *and* exhale. The inhalations are drawn deep into the lower belly and then fill up the rest of the lungs, bottom to top. The exhalations are steady and long, with a slight contraction of the abdominals toward the end, to expel all the air out. The *ujjayi* breath can be done at any time, especially when you feel the need to access and release some pent up emotional energy. It can always be used within a seated or movement meditation practice.

I love the yoga sequences with twisting poses. When you come into these deep twists, it helps to wring out the lower belly area and even more stored emotional energy will start coming up. You may have no idea what it is or what is going on. It could be old emotional wounds from childhood or new stress and tension from yesterday. All you know is that you have an intense desire to get out of the pose, resist and avoid the sensation, and hold your breath. Instead, you stay in the pose, keeping the *ujjayi* breath steady and strong. You look the sensation right in the eye and allow any anger and frustration to come up and out. Allow yourself to fully experience these emotions without holding back or resisting, as most of us have learned to do. Cry. Sob. Make any audible sounds you need to, to allow these emotions to continue surfacing and releasing. Stay in witness consciousness, observing yourself experiencing these emotions. Ride that wave of physical, mental, and emotional sensation until eventually you find yourself back in a state of peace.

When we come into a pose and take a deep breath, all of a sudden, we ask ourselves, "Ooh, what was that?" We take another deep breath, and all of a sudden we trigger sadness, frustration, irritation, or anger. We take another deep breath and find ourselves getting really upset, wanting to hold the breath so that we don't have to face these emotions. The more we work with this practice and come to understand how releasing this stored emotional energy has such a positive effect on our present experience of the world, the more apt we will be to stay with it, keep the breath deep, and wait for that emotional release. Now we feel a deep peace wash over us, and we can rest assured that one more layer of the ego has been undone.

This doesn't mean you will walk into a yoga class and everyone will be sobbing and having some sort of emotional catharsis throughout the practice. As a teacher, you may notice some students coming to tears, but some may not feel safe enough to let them go. This is why I always recommend a home practice. Once you've undone enough ego, the tears will come less and less. Even now when I practice, there are moments in which tears come. Sometimes they come because I have more stored stress to release, and sometimes they come for the sheer joy the practice brings to me.

Emotional Release in Massage

This release of emotional energy can also happen during a massage. The massage, just like a yoga pose, accesses stored emotional energy in the tissues and can draw up emotions in people that they did not realize they were holding on to.

I had a male client years ago who was about fifty at the time. I was massaging his jaw muscles, when all of a sudden, he started laughing hysterically. I had to stop and wait for him to finish. Meanwhile, I was laughing with him because his laughter was so contagious.

When he finally quit laughing, he told me that while I was sweeping my fingers through his jaw muscles, he suddenly had a vivid memory of himself as a little boy walking the halls of school. He was a little guy, so he would set his jaw in an effort to look tough, so he wouldn't get picked on by bullies. As I swept my fingers through his jaw muscles, this memory was accessed and then released through his laughter. My client was releasing forty years of energy and a memory that was still being held in his facial tissue!

I'd had clients start crying during a massage before but never laughing. It is amazing how, in a flash, a forty-year-old memory can come rising up out of nowhere with emotional energy just as potent as ever. When we realize that emotional energy attached to memories can cause unknown stress in the body and the mind, it is nice to know that we have the ability to release it through this ancient practice of yoga, releasing even more of that ego cloud.

CHAPTER 13

Samskaras: Deeply Embedded Impressions

Have I reached my full expression, or is there another defensive layer I can shed?
—Danna Faulds, excerpt from poem, "Your Full Expression" from *Poems from the Heart of Yoga* CD

Samskaras

We just looked at how the ego's thought system causes us to resist life and this resistance is then stored in the body as physical, mental, and emotional stress. But *samskaras* are a little more complex.

When our ego's resistance to life follows patterns, then this pattern of stress is now stored more deeply in the body as *samskara*. We will be looking at these *samskaras* as our deeply embedded impressions from life and the patterns and reactions these impressions then lead into. Some *samskaras* are positive or neutral, but the negative ones seem to be the most intense for us, and it will be these that we will focus on releasing. Sutra 16 in chapter 1 says, "When the ultimate level of nonreaction has been reached, pure awareness can clearly see itself as independent from the fundamental qualities of nature." (Hartranft 2006, 283-284) Learning nonreaction in regards to samskaras helps us to be able to distinguish our truest Self from the ego-self.

We can learn these patterns and reactions from parents, caretakers, or others who we are close to while growing up. We watch and learn from them and we unconsciously pick up on their emotional and physical reactions to particular situations. When a particular situation comes up in our own life that resembles one we have witnessed in the past, we can automatically go into a similar emotional pattern that we learned from a parent or caregiver and then react in ways that they may have used to deal with a similar situation.

Some *samskaras* are not learned from others but are formed from traumas of some kind in our own lives. These can be serious traumas such as abuse or not-so-serious traumas such as a childhood joke gone awry.

I'll share several different examples of how we can acquire *samskaras* and the habitual reactions they then cause us to act out in response to similar stressors.

Example 1

When my niece was two years old, my sister brought her over to my house around Halloween. I had this really scary mask that looked like Freddy Krueger. Without realizing, I put the mask on when my niece wasn't looking, so when she turned around, all she saw was this scary person walking toward her. She immediately started screaming and crying and buried her head in a chair. I went running to her as I took off the mask and tried to make her understand. She was in terror; not even my sister could calm her down.

Of course I felt terrible, but the worst part was that she was terrified of any masks from that point on: Batman, clown, you name it. Halloween, for the next several years, was hard on my sister and especially my niece. This initial trauma of seeing me in that mask created a deeply embedded impression and pattern of fear that came up every time she saw another mask. This then triggered that reaction of "avoidance at all costs" of the present particular stressor, even when it seemed totally illogical. This avoidance was meant to "save" her from

> The impression of *samskara* is so deeply embedded, so deeply etched in our memory, that when the pattern repeats and the reaction is triggered in an effort to protect us, no logic can stop it. Fight or flight has kicked in.

the stressor, since avoidance "saved" her in the past from the initial scary mask. The impression of *samskara* is so deeply embedded, so deeply etched in our memory, that when the pattern repeats and the reaction is triggered in an effort to protect us, no logic can stop it. Fight or flight has kicked in.

Example 2

When I was a kid, my brother would pin me down, poke me in the chest, and ask, "Do you smoke, do you smoke?" It was supposed to be some torturous way to get a kid to admit to something they weren't supposed to be doing, like smoking cigarettes. But it made me laugh hysterically, even though I was in an extreme amount of pain on a lot of different levels: pain that I was being pinned down and I couldn't do anything about it, pain from the poking in the chest, and pain from not being able to get him back.

Years later, when I was in massage school, I learned that tickling was the first sign of pain. I believed that, because when my brother had me pinned down, it was an extremely painful experience. It brought up a lot of rage at the time, disguised underneath the hysterical laughing. As my brother grew up and moved out, I never really thought about it until I had my first boyfriend in college years later. He went to tickle me at some point, and without even realizing I was going to do it, I slapped him. Of course, he was upset. But in that moment, I realized all of that rage, anger, and vulnerability I had felt when my brother pinned me down all those years ago came roaring back up inside me like a flash.

My brother is a wonderful guy, so there was nothing mean or hateful in his pinning me down. He was just being an older brother. But this flash of memory, this impression, evoked an immediate pattern of deeply embedded emotions of rage and vulnerability. This triggered a reactionary response of slapping my boyfriend, something I had always wanted or tried to do to my brother all those years ago, in an effort to protect myself. After that, I always warned people and told them I wasn't responsible for what I may do to them if they tickled me. I really didn't feel like I could stop the sudden rage or the reaction that came with it.

Example 3

Watching my mom night after night reenact the nightly dramas set a deep *samskara* within me. As I mentioned before, I was super-sensitive to acts of betrayal, not only in my own relationship but also in others around me. Whenever I encountered a partner even remotely being flirtatious with another girl, it triggered deep patterns of emotional pain in the form of extreme sadness, insecurity, fear, anger, and a feeling that I was completely and utterly alone. This usually ended in various reactions depending on the situation, but many were clearly reactions I had learned firsthand from these nightly dramas.

Think of *samskaras* as the ego keeping us on its track to nowhere. Because now, instead of being fully immersed in the experience of each moment in life, we are basically living in emotions from the past that continuously come up as the present reminds us of the past. Now we find ourselves continuously reacting in the same ways that we did in the past. We get stuck following these same old reactions, because the ego tricks us into thinking that this reaction has "saved" us in the past in a similar situation, so this same reaction must be able to save us now. There is a level of self-preservation embedded in this *samskara*. On a deep level, we truly believe these patterns and the subsequent automatic reactions are literally keeping us alive. This is what makes *samskaras* so difficult to release, especially when we are totally unaware of them.

By learning to release *samskaras,* now we are taking ourselves off the path the ego has laid out for us, the path of not truly experiencing life or enjoying it. When we learn to reidentify ourselves in our true nature as eternal Spirit, unable to die, then the deeply embedded idea that these *samskaras* are responsible for our self-preservation is no longer meaningful or necessary. We realize that this self-preservation is only the preservation of the false self or ego. When you recognize that you are eternal Spirit, all connected, all One, there is nothing to save you from. There is no need for self-preservation and no need for *samskara*.

How do we begin to release *samskaras* when they are so deeply etched in our memories and so automatic that they seem next to impossible to stop? We begin with yoga.

Yoga and *Samskaras*

Samskaras can hide so deeply within our psyches that we have to have some sort of process to bring them back up so that we can release them. Yoga is this process. Yoga practice makes it easy to access the emotional energy and pattern of samskara, without it being as intense as a real-life trigger, which can throw us into that automatic fight-or-flight reaction.

Initially, yoga helps to release the *samskaric* pattern by releasing the stored mental and emotional stress causing us to be vulnerable to *samskaras*. Think of this stress (this physical and mental tension, uncomfortable emotions, and feelings of resistance) as physical and mental noise. Most of us go through life ignoring this noise and utilizing any distractions to keep us from having to face it. Many of us know that we are uncomfortable or even suffering, but we are not aware enough to realize that the discomfort is due to our ignoring the mental and emotional stress.

When we practice yoga, we tune in to this stress, this ego noise in the body and the mind. We tune in to the body's discomforts in the form of tight hamstrings or a tight lower back. We "ride the wave" of sensation, the hallmark of Kripalu Yoga, as we tune in to the emotion attached to that physical tension, such as anger or sadness, whatever it may be, and breathe through it. As we tune in to the noise fully and breathe through it, we experience it fully, instead of resisting it. Now we can allow it to move through us and release. As this ego noise is released, the mind is turned over to Spirit and we experience quiet mind. From here we are open and tuned into our higher guidance.

When I teach, I love to read a portion of one of Danna Faulds's poems from her CD, *Poems from the Heart of Yoga*, called "Your Full Expression." One line of the poem asks the question: "Have I reached my full expression, or is there another defensive layer I can shed?" (Faulds 2011)

As we come into yoga poses, we ask ourselves, "Have I come into my full expression?" In other words, am I accessing stored physical, mental, emotional tension and stress? If not, maybe I can go deeper into this pose and find this stored stress, find another defensive layer of ego that is ready to be undone.

Once we have released enough of this emotional stress during yoga practice, there isn't enough stress to drive the *samskaric* pattern and reaction *as* automatically and *as* quickly as it once did. The real test is when our *samskaras* are triggered by something in daily life. When a situation or circumstance comes up that reminds us subconsciously of the past, instead of automatically going into that *samskara* and reacting from ego, now we have time to take a deep breath, stay in peace, and make a different choice as to how we handle this situation. Now we have *slowed down* enough to access witness consciousness in the midst of the pattern. From here, the mind is quieter, and we can tune in more easily to our intuition, our higher self guiding us to make a different choice.

With our higher self's guidance, we bring the samskaric pattern to consciousness. We choose not to let the pattern take over, but rather to observe the pattern and allow ourselves to experience fully *all* the different emotions that come with it. As these emotions related to the samskaric pattern are then released, we are no longer driven into our habitual reaction. As yoga says, we begin to fill in the groove of the *samskara*. We have now brought the samskara into consciousness and it can no longer have the same effect on us. The more we practice, the less these triggers can affect us, until eventually the *samskara* is undone completely.

Once you have been working with these *samskaras*, you will notice the ego kicking and screaming like a two-year-old having a tantrum. It will put you through every thought and emotion it can muster up to send you back into those habitual patterns and reactions. It can be tough because we are creatures of habit, and the ego tempts us into thinking that it is more comfortable to move into these old samskaric patterns and reactions. If you can really sink into witness consciousness and move through the process of simply observing what's happening, experiencing any emotions coming up, and then allowing them to release, the end result will be worth your while. Now you have stopped the pattern and dealt with it before the reaction has begun. *Voila!* Embarrassing reaction averted!

Stephen Cope, in his book *The Wisdom of Yoga,* says the following: "Here is the kicker: when they [meaning *samskaras*] are re-experienced without reactivity—with a balance of awareness and equanimity—they are digested, burned up, or as yogis sometimes say, 'cooked'—just as digestion burns up a big meal" (Cope 2006, 198–199).

In time, the more and more we practice, the more ego is released, and soon we find ourselves perfectly at peace, no matter what triggers may be showing up around us. We now are no longer being tricked and tempted by the ego into allowing it to control our minds and rule our lives with deeply stored patterns of emotions and subsequent reactions. Yoga has now taken us off the ego's emotional roller coaster and the ego's path to nowhere.

Sometimes you may find that when a situation comes up that is bringing up a particular *samskara* in you, you still choose to react in your habitual way. That's okay! This is a process. Simply slowing down and being able to observe yourself going into the emotional pattern and then making the wrong choice to stay in it and react from it is a step in the right direction. Remember, the ego is tricky. It loves a good fight, and it loves to stay in its comfort zone. When it takes over despite your best attempts, forgive it and move on. These deep patterns of *samskara* take time to fill in. But when they come up, they will only help increase your compassion for others when their ego takes over too. In the meantime, yoga helps us let go of the ego thoughts, beliefs, and emotional energy driving these *samskaras*, uncovering our defensive layers and shedding them one by one.

Having Fun Tracking *Samskara*

I want to give you an example of being able to track *samskara* showing up in your life in subtle ways and becoming more aware of how easily we can create *samskaras* in our children.

I give you a typical morning at my house.
I am running late. I'm going to be late getting my child to school, and her teacher is not going to be happy with me. Then my blood pressure goes up, and my child is taking forever putting on her shoes. The stress and anger rises until all of a sudden I yell, "Hurry up!"

She starts crying. I feel guilty for upsetting her. My neck and shoulders are in knots, and the kicker is, now I am going to be even later, because now I have to take the time to sit down and explain why Mommy yelled, apologize, and wait for her forgiveness, all the while wondering how it could ever be worth it to yell at my child over the simple reason of running late.

I realize that this precious child doesn't understand the meaning of time and running late, and that is, for the most part, why she is so happy and joyful and content in life. Now I am simply teaching her how to stress over time, which now seems completely unimportant in the grand scheme of things.

My ongoing yoga practice enabled me to slow down and go into witness consciousness so that I could track the thought patterns that were arising and causing the anger and stress. I was able to slow down enough to notice a negative voice in my head telling me I was worthless or disrespectful for being late. "You have to be punctual, or you are being disrespectful. This is all your fault. If you weren't so lazy and worthless, you would have gotten up earlier, and none of this would be happening." I was witnessing the samskara in action.

Once I tracked these reactions back to these long-held learned thought patterns, simply shining the light on them caused them to let go and lose their effect on me. Now the guilt, feelings of inadequacy and fear which normally accompanied the thought pattern, no longer had enough weight for them to drive that stress reaction of getting angry and yelling. As I kept breathing and stayed present, I was able to release the emotional energy and clear out these *samskaras*, rather than allowing them to throw me into that habitual pattern of emotion and the subsequent reaction.

You can have a lot of fun figuring out what your own *samskaras* are— the more obvious ones and the less obvious ones. That's the key. Don't get too serious when you are working with these. This is how the ego works. We all are subjected to it, but there is a way out. It's a lot of fun to be able to keep your sense of humor as you watch yourself going into these habitual patterns of emotion and reaction, eventually getting to a place where you can let these patterns go.

Seeing *Samskara* in others

You may know someone who deals with a particularly difficult *samskara*. You may see them go into that pattern and then react in the same way over and over again. If you can be patient and understand that this pattern feels virtually impossible for them to get out of, then you can help by not then reacting yourself. As you stay calm and keep sending them peace and love through the mind, they will calm much more quickly and quite possibly be able to release it eventually. In a later chapter we will get into forgiveness and being able to hold the truth in your mind for people. Remember, we all deal with this made-up ego mental construct. As long as you can remember that we are all one: whole, perfect, and eternal, then you can help others to remember that too.

My Biggest Lesson with *Samskara*

My relationship with my ex-husband was the first relationship in which my *samskaras* learned from my childhood really surfaced. At that time, I drank to excess, so there were a few nights on which I thought he was flirty with other girls. This triggered those same feelings of betrayal that my mom had experienced all those years ago. Interestingly enough, when I talked to my mom about it, she was able to see that I was overreacting. But just like her many years ago, because I was in it, I could *see* that I was overreacting, but I felt I had no control to be able to stop it.

The bottom line was that I never felt good enough. With my own extreme intoxication most weekends when I went out, whatever fears I had were exacerbated by the alcohol and/or drugs I had consumed. I was feeding the monster! This ugliness inside emerged: a combination of a woman scorned (for the record, my ex never cheated, just my drama playing out); the jealous bitch; and the terribly frightened, achingly sad and lonely child I once was. Yikes!

I was eaten up with jealousy and insecurity and the fear that my ex would someday hurt me. I expected him to betray me and almost wanted him to, so I could get it over with and submerge myself in the pity and loneliness that had plagued me for so long, proving to myself that I really was as unworthy as I felt.

A part of me enjoyed these feelings of inadequacy and isolation. I sometimes felt like it was me against the world. I was comfortable in this misery because I was used to it. It was what I learned and what I knew, the same things my mom had learned from her mom. Nevertheless, overall it was still miserable and suffocating.

Now I understood how my mom was able to drag out the drama night after night all those years ago. A part of her wanted to let it go, but the ego, with all of its fear and insecurity, was too deeply engrained for her to be able to stop it initially. On a much deeper level, she needed to fully experience all her fears. She needed to immerse herself fully in hell to be able to emerge at some point with the realization that there was a part of her (her true nature) that could not be hurt or negatively altered in any way. I now understood that sometimes we have to go through hell and face our worst fears head on to finally come full circle to the realization that there is an aspect of self, our true nature, that cannot be harmed by anything of this world. When our ego feels pretty banged up and bruised, we can still tap into our truest nature as eternal Spirit that has not been altered in the least.

> When our ego feels pretty banged up and bruised, we can still tap into our truest nature as eternal Spirit that has not been altered in the least.

When I was faced with my parents' divorce, I had to take a long look at the *samskara* that was repeating, not just in my relationship with my ex but in my relationship with my mom. I was always taking things out on my mom as payback for what I felt she had put us through. Payback we had learned from her as she made my dad pay. Payback she had learned from my grandmother as my grandmother made my grandfather pay. There was a deeply held pattern of blame based on fear that needed to be let go of. Ah, *samskara!*

The deep heart openers and backbends helped me to release a lot of my *samskaras*. In the first few years of my practice, while in poses such as *danurasana*, bow pose, and *ustrasana*, camel pose, I had a lot of anxiety come up—anxiety and stress from all those years ago as a child, watching the nightly drama unfold within my house. My pectoral muscles were extremely tight and shortened from many years of hunching over, guarding my heart and chest. These heart-opener poses brought up a feeling of restriction around my heart and throat, a feeling like I couldn't breathe, I couldn't relax. It took literally several years, but finally I reached a point in which I could come into these poses comfortably, without any old stored emotional energy coming up. I had finally released it all! The best part about it was that it was positively affecting my day-to-day life enormously. My deep anger and fear of getting hurt in relationships was fading. I knew I would be okay no matter what.

This practice enabled me to look at my mother and what she went through with more clarity and less judgment and anger on my part. That's when I realized how strong my mother was. All she wanted, like any of us ever want, was to feel loved. Her mother never made her feel that way, her husband fell for another woman, and her kids blamed her constantly for her mistakes. But she was still kicking. I realized that it was time to let go of all the blame and judgment I had been holding over my mom's head all those years. It was time to let go of the past and see my mother as whole, perfect, and eternal and love her unconditionally.

Mom now is in the best place emotionally that I have ever seen her. I can now fully enjoy our relationship, knowing that I no longer blame or judge her or myself for past actions based on fear and insecurity. We have always had a great relationship, but I would say that now it is the best it ever was.

Simple Yet Complex

If all we have to do is to remember in every moment that we are eternal Spirit in order to find fulfillment, this sounds fairly easy. The ego makes it tricky. We have so much stored in our minds and our bodies from past hurts and traumas, no matter how big or how tiny, and they all are having an effect on our present experience in the world. These are the aspects of ego that we have to work on releasing.

It will not be easy to face everything we are holding on to from past hurts, guilt, and shame that may be looming over us like a big shadow, but we must stay disciplined to stay with the process and allow it to open us up for forgiveness, freedom, unconditional love, peace, and joy. Once you begin undoing the ego, you'll start to find that you are letting things go in life that are no longer serving you, that have been unknowingly reinforcing your pain and stress. For example, you may start eating healthier. You may let go of a straining exercise regimen that you have been forcing yourself to do for years. You may let go of some unhealthy relationships.

> It will not be easy to face everything we are holding on to from past hurts, guilt, and shame that may be looming over us like a big shadow, but we must stay disciplined to stay with the process and allow it to open us up for forgiveness, freedom, unconditional love, peace, and joy.

You realize that you are ready to let go of anything that brings more stress into your life.

Now you are taking responsibility for the life you want to live.

CHAPTER 14

Witness Consciousness vs. True Nature & Step 3 to Awakening

As long as we can objectively observe our thoughts and feelings, division remains, but when there is perfect unity, this observing is no longer possible.

—Bernadette Roberts, *The Path to No-Self: Life at the Center* (Roberts 1991, 52)

Witness Consciousness vs. Our True Nature

Don't confuse *witness consciousness* with *our true nature*. Witness consciousness is a very peaceful, observant state, but one in which we are still conscious of separation. As we learn to stay focused in this peaceful state, we will be guided by our higher self to make choices based on Spirit rather than ego. Eventually, our higher self utilizes this peaceful state to take us beyond witness consciousness, beyond choice, and into what yoga calls pure awareness. So once we have identified witness consciousness, there is still another step to our true nature.

Living a life awake is living from witness consciousness part of the time and your true nature part of the time, aware of your higher self in both. In witness consciousness you

> Living a life awake is living from witness consciousness part of the time and your true nature part of the time, aware of your higher self in both. In witness consciousness you become consciously aware of your ego-self and your higher self, and in your true nature you are simply *in the experience* of your higher self.

become consciously aware of your ego-self and your higher self, and in your true nature you are simply *in the experience* of your higher self.

Bernadette Roberts is a Christian contemplative and a former Carmelite nun. She left the order and raised a family as she continued on her contemplative path and wrote three books about her journey to awakening. I'm going to share a passage from her book called *The Path to No-Self: Life at the Center.*

> By remaining passive, however, we learn the knack of being objective about our thoughts and feelings, and come to see them for what they are—superficial. Without depth, perishable, fickle, disturbers of peace, and totally incompatible with life at the center. As long as we can objectively observe our thoughts and feelings, division remains, but when there is perfect unity, this observing is no longer possible. (Roberts 1991, 52)

Here, she is talking about what yoga calls *witness consciousness* and how we have to go beyond witness consciousness, beyond the observant state, to truly go beyond separation to the experience of our perfect unity.

Because it feels as if we are about to step off a ledge and let go of our selves completely, full awakening can be a little scary at this point. Once we do, there is nothing scary about it, and we have all done it plenty of times without realizing. Full awakening is as simple as utilizing witness consciousness to shift out of our ego-self and the made-up ego mental construct, and then letting go of witness consciousness (consciousness altogether) as we drop into what yoga calls *pure awareness* (the experience of our true nature as Spirit). Now we are *in* the experience of life again, just like when we were babies. We no longer simply experience life, because (for this particular moment as long as it may last) we have let go of the self completely. No more thoughts, beliefs, judgments, or resistances to the experience of life.

As long as we are still working on detaching from the ego, we will need choices, practices, processes, and the occasional withdrawal from situations that keep us stuck in the ego's thought system in order to set ourselves free.

As long as we are still working on detaching from the ego, we will need choices, practices, processes, and the occasional withdrawal from situations that keep us stuck in the ego's thought system in order to set ourselves free.

114

Savasana

Most of us cannot live in the state of pure awareness indefinitely. We flip-flop back and forth, and that's okay. We simply continue to trust this ability to step off the ledge again and again and really let ourselves go. This is why the guided relaxations and *savasana* are so important. *Savasana* is the relaxation pose at the end of a yoga class in which you lie down and simply relax. The poses during a yoga practice prepare us for *savasana* by alleviating some of the discomforts in the body, focusing the mind on something other than our habitual ways of thinking and analyzing, and releasing stored emotional stress. The yoga practice enables us to let go of enough ego so that when it is time for *savasana*, the body is in a very relaxed state and the mind is ready to let go of its focus completely. Now we can go beyond the mind and the body and drop into this pure awareness, this experience of our true nature as Spirit quite easily.

I had two particular students in class before: one who would leave early once it was time for *savasana* and another who would lie there and move constantly. I was pretty sure they were both clinging to what they needed to go do after class. It was clear that neither was able to simply relax enough to let go. After months and months, I noticed the one beginning to stay for *savasana* and the other one eventually was able to lie still and let go into the relaxation. It took time, but the practice eventually enabled them to let go enough of that stored emotional stress so that they could step off that ledge when it came time for *savasana*.

Savasana is our time to let go for a short while of who we are in this lifetime and all the responsibilities and to-do lists we need to check off for the day. It may take us awhile before we can truly let go long enough to allow ourselves to go beyond the body and beyond the mind into the experience of deep relaxation that is our true nature. Stepping off that ledge of witness consciousness into an experience of deep peace and relaxation as pure awareness, is worth the wait. As we re-awaken from *savasana*, we bring Spirit's deep, restorative peace with us. We feel relaxed, renewed, and recharged.

Practice as a Means to "Get Present" Rather than "Exercise."

I've mentioned that yoga works on us in two ways: the first is the undoing of the ego, or thinning out that ego cloud, and the second is actually rising above that ego cloud entirely. We can undo the ego all we want, but until we really understand and utilize the self-study and practices to shift out of the ego, we will just simply continue to build more ego even as we are releasing it. In my initial yoga practice, I was letting go of a lot of my ego, as that stored emotional stress. But, because I was driving myself to be able to get into certain poses and practice certain routines each day, I was also unknowingly building more ego at the same time. The practice was still about "exercise" and what my body could do, rather than serving as a means to get present and experience my true nature.

When I first began going to yoga classes, I always wondered how yoga teachers became so limber so quickly. I wondered if they practiced before class to loosen up. When I first became a teacher, I actually did practice before class to warm up a bit. In 2010, I went to a workshop with Shiva Rea, who is a big-time yoga teacher who travels all over the world teaching. One day after class, I asked her how much she had to practice daily to keep her body as strong and flexible as it was. I wanted to know what her routine was. She never answered my question. She said, "Oh, what a wonderful question. Why don't you ask me again when the group comes back?" I never asked the question when the group came back.

A few months later, I realized why I had never asked that question again. I realized that I had to find this answer out for myself. This particular workshop with Shiva Rea was called "Embodying the Flow," and although I had always done flow yoga, this workshop was what I needed to really "step off that ledge." It allowed me to let go of the drive to practice certain poses and simply allow myself to flow through the practice.

When I could step off this ledge during my yoga practice, it took me into the present so automatically that there was little warm-up needed, even for the more difficult poses. That's when the concept of yoga as a means to simply get present—not as exercise—really sank in for me. What I found for myself was that I enjoyed the practice even more when my ego wasn't driving it to be a certain way, when I had the freedom to let myself flow with no expected outcome. Ultimately, I realized that if I could easily step off this ledge in my practice, I could just as easily step off this ledge in daily life. By doing so, I allowed myself to flow through my day rather than let the ego drive me through it.

Beyond the Practice—True Surrender

Once we can rest in our true nature automatically, there is no need for practice. The practice is now our life. There are people out there who are living in their true nature in every moment. For some people, the ego still may come up, but they automatically Choose Spirit Now and choose to step back off that ledge into that peaceful state of Spirit. For others, the ego is completely undone and they are beyond having to make a choice. They have stepped off that ledge and are fully immersed in their true nature as Spirit, as peace, unconditional love, and joy. They are fully in the experience of life, and absolutely nothing can trigger them to fall back into the ego-self and it's thought system.

Story about Swami Kripalu and His Teacher, Gurudev

I have a beautiful story to share with you about Swami Kripalu and his teacher, Gurudev. This story is from Atma Jo Ann Levitt's book again, *The Pilgrim of Love: The Life and Teaching of Swami Kripalu*. One day, Kripalu is asking his teacher why he has to chant the mantra "Om Namah Shivaya" (or, "Lord, Shiva, I surrender myself to you") over and over again. "Won't he understand the first time?" Kripalu asks (Levitt 2004, 41).

His teacher, Gurudev, tells him, "God is so merciful, that if you say it just once, he will accept it. But your mind is so cunning, that even saying it hundreds of times, you still don't mean it. That is why you have to repeat it over and over. When the mind truly surrenders to the Lord, you don't have to do any *japa*" (Levitt 2004, 41–42). *Japa* is simply repeating a particular mantra over and over.

When people pray, it's not about, "Hey God, remember me down here? Help!"

> What praying does and what this whole process of awakening does is to remind *us* of God, to remind *us* that we are a part of God, that God is a part of us, and that there is no separating the two.

What praying does and what this whole process of awakening does is to remind *us* of God, to remind *us* that we are a part of God, that God is a part of us, and that there is no separating the two. It is for us to remember what we really want in life: to stop searching in all the wrong places for things that don't bring us lasting happiness; to find that awakening; to wake up to our true nature as Spirit, unconditionally loving, peaceful, joyful, happy, and fulfilled; to find ourselves in a place ego cannot drag us back out of, a place in which we remember in every moment this eternal connection with God. Until we find ourselves living in this state of awakening all the time, we continue to keep up with the process, with the practices, and with prayer. It all helps us to remember what is really important until we no longer need the reminder. Once we are awake, we no longer need to practice or pray, because now *every moment is our practice*, every moment is our prayer if we remember, in every moment, that we are eternally connected with God.

> Once we are awake, we no longer need to practice or pray, because now *every moment is our practice*, every moment is our prayer if we remember, in every moment, that we are eternally connected with God.

Step Three to Awakening: Detach from the Ego as the Self

Step 3 to awakening is to detach from thinking the ego is our true self. Witness consciousness allows us to move through step 3 easily. As we shift into witness consciousness and tune in to this peaceful place inside, we begin to notice that it is separate from the ego thoughts and noise going on in the mind and we begin naturally detaching from our notion of self as this ego. We detach from our notion of self as the impermanent body, the thoughts running rampant in our head, and the false self-image

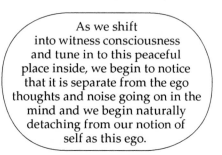

> As we shift into witness consciousness and tune in to this peaceful place inside, we begin to notice that it is separate from the ego thoughts and noise going on in the mind and we begin naturally detaching from our notion of self as this ego.

we've been building and creating all our lives. As we become more established in witness consciousness we naturally detach from the ego the more we study and observe it non-judgmentally. In step three, the ego cloud surrounding us is beginning to disappear, the made-up ego mental construct is beginning to disassemble, and we are well aware that we are more than this ego-self that we have been limiting ourselves to.

Welcome to the gentle awakening.

In the next chapter we will go in depth as to how the ego self-image is built from the ground up. This will open our eyes even more to our false sense of self and allow us to move through this step 3, detaching from the ego, much more easily.

CHAPTER 15

Building the Ego's Self-Image

As soon as you believe that a label you've put on yourself
is true, you've limited something that is literally limitless,
you've limited who you are into nothing more than a thought.
—Adyashanti, *Falling into Grace* (2010, 19)

Ego Clouds Our True Nature as Perfection

Somewhere deep inside, we know the truth. In our true nature as One, we are equally special and perfect. But the ego has clouded our vision. It has made us forget our Oneness, our connection, our specialness, and perfection as God created us. Within the ego's thought system, "specialness" and "perfection" are something we don't already have, or if we do, it's something that can be taken away. Now the ego drives us to attain and maintain this "specialness" and "perfection" by building it through our false self-image. We are always coming up short because our striving is based on the ego's definition of perfection, and that is based on separation, competition, and the desire to be better than others.

This perfection is no longer about our perfection as One. It is about being more perfect than another, more special than somebody else. As long as we desire to be "better" than others, we are at the mercy of the ego. Our true nature as One in Spirit is true perfection because there is no desire to be better than another. Trying to be better than another has absolutely no meaning. Even being equal has no meaning in our true nature because as One, there is no other to be equal to.

How do we begin building this false ego self-image that ends up clouding our vision of the truth?

Building Self-Image

As children, we are taught who we are by our parents, our friends' parents, our siblings, relatives, and friends. We learn the "rules of this world" and get a vague idea of what we look like to others and then innately try and build on this as we grow up.

As a kid, I remember overhearing parents of my friends telling my mom that I was "so sweet" and "just an angel." I remember that even though I didn't feel that way inside, I felt like I had to keep making them think it was true, so I made more of an effort to be "sweet" around them. This is how that self-image starts. We hear someone labeling us, and we either strive to prove them right or strive to prove them wrong. We are constantly striving to live up to expectations we think others have placed on us and that we have then placed on ourselves.

We do our best to mold ourselves into what we think we are supposed to be, most of us not realizing that we are getting angry and resentful in the process. We spend a great deal of time and energy trying to be what we think people expect us to be, trying to build a self-image that fits into our world. At some point, we wake up to find that we are not living the life we want to live.

Some of you may know Mr. Nice Guy. Everyone talks about how "nice" this person is, and they expect him to be super-nice all the time. At some point, Mr. Nice Guy may feel disingenuous and end up feeling resentful or even angry because he has bound himself to this self-image. He may fear letting people down who expect this of him, so he spends a lot of energy trying to keep up this façade.

When Mr. Nice Guy really looks at these unrealistic expectations he and society have placed upon him, he wonders if he can let them go and be true to himself and to what he really wants in life. This will allow him to let go of all the pent-up emotion that has been suppressed. This Mr. Nice Guy is an example of a self-image that the ego has created, a *nice* self-image but still a *false* self-image born out of the ego's thought system.

In most cases, we spend so much time and effort building our self-image that we lose touch with and forget all about our true nature. We identify solely with this self-image, cling on to this image, and live in fear of anything changing or blemishing our self-image in any way. Here we experience all the negative emotions such as stress and fear that this misidentification with the ego brings, and we find ourselves in a state in which we are spiritually starved.

> A self-image is nothing more than a collection of thoughts and beliefs about ourselves, the expectations based on these thoughts and beliefs, and the subsequent ego-driven actions which are meant to uphold these expectations.

A self-image is nothing more than a collection of thoughts and beliefs about ourselves, the expectations based on these thoughts and beliefs, and the subsequent ego-driven actions which are meant to uphold these expectations. For instance, people who have been told that they are "worthless" and "no good" all their lives might constantly push themselves to gain affection. They might also live lethargically, because they truly believe they *are* worthless and no good. Our self-image is kept alive in our minds; it is responsible for driving us in particular ways, depending on what thoughts and expectations our particular self-image was built upon.

If you take the time to shine the light on your own self-image, you might notice how fickle it can be as your thoughts move from ones that build you up (imagine your most confident self-image) to those that tear you down (imagine your most insecure self-image). Notice how fickle you feel about your friend when you think of him or her in a positive way and then again in a negative way. Our images and impressions of ourselves and others are dependent on our thoughts and beliefs. They can change as swiftly as our mind flits from one thing to another. Not only is it silly for us to put any stock in these self-images, it's really not fair to ourselves and others to see each other through such unfair, judgmental, and arbitrary ego eyeglasses. Let's take those suckers off!

When I was twenty-eight, I divorced my ex-husband. Fortunately at that point in my life, I realized that worrying about what others thought was useless. No one but me had to live my life, and at that point, I was determined to start living it the way I wanted. I then realized that the belief that others really sat around talking about me or about how I was living my life was a very egocentric thought. Surely, people had better things to talk about!

If people do care how we are living our lives, then they are either our mothers or they are most likely the ones who are not living the way they really want to. In most cases, even though people may be talking negatively about us, if we are following our intuition, we are serving as a real positive role model. One day, the ones who were gossiping about us might be able to see and learn from that.

Self-Image as Labels on Ourselves

A part of building a self-image is labeling yourself.

"I'm a pretty nice person."
"I'm a Republican."
"I'm a Democrat."
"I'm not good at public speaking."

As Adyashanti says in his book, *Falling into Grace*, "As soon as you believe that a label you've put on yourself is true, you've limited something that is literally limitless, you've limited who you are into nothing more than a thought" (2010, 19).

In our true nature, we are this eternal Spirit with limitless creative ability and limitless connection with everything in creation. As we build our ego self-image and begin to label ourselves, we take away all these other possibilities that we could be in life. So this is a powerful and consequential statement right here.

Think of every label you have for yourself as another limiting belief you have placed upon yourself. A label is simply a judgment in disguise. Even though it may be a positive label, it is still a judgment about yourself or another. So think back to Mr. Nice Guy. You may tell Mr. Nice Guy how sweet he is all the time. Without realizing it, you are pressuring him with that judgment, that label, into thinking he has to keep up this façade, even though it's a positive one.

Notice the freedom and the lack of judgment of yourself and others when those labels are shed, even the good ones. This is where non-attachment comes in again. To a certain degree, we need labels. If you strike up a conversation with somebody and they ask you who you are and what you do, you're probably not going to say, "Well, I can't really tell you right now because I'm really working on letting go of my self-image and trying not to label myself." That person you're talking to is probably going to turn around and run as fast as possible in the opposite direction! To a certain degree, we need labels to communicate with others, but we can let go of the ones that are holding us back. We can detach from our *misidentification of self* with the labels we still use for communication.

Getting Out of the Box

Growing up, I went to a private school. I was in this box of like-minded people who dressed a certain way and thought a certain way. When I was in my twenties, I began meeting people who were totally different and thought in so many different ways. It was a very refreshing experience. It was amazing to begin shedding the old labels and old thought systems I had about myself and others. However, in hindsight, I realized that as I began shedding these old labels, I was then picking up new ones. And even more, as I picked up these new ones, I then began to judge the old ones.

I was raised Republican, and all my life, I heard judgments about the Democrats. But in my twenties, when I decided to label myself a Democrat, I found I was judging the Republicans. I noticed this happening with several different labels I was trying out. When I became "spiritual and non-religious" rather than religious, I was judging religions and religious people. This isn't right either. So when you decide to say "this is what I am" and label yourself, whether you mean it or not, you are limiting yourself. Anyone who labels themselves as the opposite feels judged by you on some level. Simply be aware of labels as judgments in disguise.

Once we build our self-image and begin labeling ourselves, we spend an enormous amount of energy and effort keeping up the façade. What makes the ego mental construct so complex is that there is so much that plays into it and reinforces it, yet it is really only an illusion. It gets even more complicated when our attention gets distracted and the ego pulls out all of its tricks to keep us immersed in its mental construct. In the next chapter, we will learn the ego's tricks and temptations so that we can be more aware of how the ego keeps us immersed in its cloud.

CHAPTER 16

Yoga: Shining Light on the Ego's Tricks & Temptations

And at its [ego] altar, it demands you lay all of the things it
bids you get, leaving you no joy in them. (ACIM T-13.VII.10:13)

Kleshas: Afflictions in the Mind in Yoga
(aka Ego Tricks or Temptations)

Once we establish our ego-self, thought system and false self-image,
we are bound by ego consciousness and it is easy to get stuck here and
forget there is a way out. We will now take a look at the *kleshas,* the
Sanskrit word for what yoga calls the afflictions of the mind. Unless we
learn what to look out for, *kleshas* are the ego mind tricks or temptations
that keep us immersed in this negative ego thought system and belief
system. Some are tricky, in that we don't realize what is happening.
Some are tempting, in that we realize what is happening but are
tempted by them nonetheless. Remember how Jesus and the Buddha
went through a period of intense temptation before they awakened or
enlightened? Listen up!

What I love about the *kleshas* is that they are just as true for us today
as they were for those yogis four thousand years ago when they were
first written about in the Vedas and then two thousand years ago when
they were written about again in the Yoga Sutras. We have learned that
yoga establishes witness consciousness, and this witness consciousness
allows us to slow down enough to look at and study these ego mind
tricks and temptations as they become apparent in our own daily lives.

We will go through each of the five *kleshas* one by one.

1. Ignorance: *avidya*
2. Ego: *asmita*
3. Attachment or attraction: *raga*
4. Avoidance or aversion: *dvesha*
5. Fear of death: *abhinivesah*

We will also discuss delusion, or *moha*, which can be seen as a more intense form of avoidance. It is not listed as one of the five kleshas in the sutras but is said to give rise to unwholesome thoughts, ignorance and suffering.

I call these the "ego mind tricks," but the other culprit for all these other afflictions is also ignorance (*avidya*). When you take a look at ignorance (*avidya*) and ego (*asmita*), these two really seem to go hand in hand. As our parents "see" us into this world and establish our false self (ego), we begin to forget our underlying connection with everything (ignorance). Ego (*asmita*) and ignorance (*avidya*) seem to coincide with each other and eventually drive the other afflictions of the mind, which in turn enmesh us into ego and ignorance even further. Does the term "vicious cycle" come to mind?

Ignorance as a Major Ego Trick

Avidya is ignorance, no knowledge of who and what we really are. Often you will find the *kleshas* listed as five afflictions of the mind with *avidya*, ignorance of who and what we are, being responsible for the ego and all the other afflictions. Ignorance is not always bliss!

Ignorance (*avidya*) allows us to get totally immersed in the ego's thought system, the false self, so completely that we forget that there is a true part of ourselves that we are missing. As long as we are ignorant of the ego and its ability to keep us in the dark, we will *remain* in the dark until we finally hit a breaking point. We will experience dissatisfaction, pain and suffering, and unhappiness and unfulfillment with no knowledge that there is a way out of suffering. Immersion in the ego's thought system and belief system perpetuates ignorance (*avidya*); it's like a vicious cycle.

God, the Divine, is watching out for us. Our higher self *is* watching out for us. Even if we are immersed completely, at some point, we *will* notice our inner guidance. It may take some of us a lot longer, but eventually, we will *all* be led out of ignorance and into the light of awakening. When we find ourselves at a breaking point, that is usually when we fall down on our knees and ask for help. This is okay. Sometimes it takes hitting rock bottom for us to finally ask for help. Now Holy Spirit can get through and show you the way. Once you understand that there is a way out, once you understand that you are experiencing your false ego-self (but that you *can* experience your true nature), you are on your path—and there is no way off the path.

Once you come out of this ignorance even a little bit, you can never be re-immersed completely. At times, it may feel like you are re-immersed completely, but deep inside, you know the truth. You know that you can eventually pull yourself out, with the help of your higher self. Remember, God loves us unconditionally, and with unconditional love comes total freedom. We have to have that "little willingness" that the Course speaks of to ask for help from within when we are ready to break out of the ego's thought system.

Cultivate Knowledge

In yoga there is a practice called *cultivating opposites*. In chapter 2 of the *Yoga Sutras*, Sutra 33 says, "Unwholesome thoughts can be neutralized by cultivating wholesome ones." (Hartranft 2006, 287) The opposite of ignorance is knowledge, so cultivate knowledge of the truth. We are going to choose to take programs like Choose Spirit Now. We are going to choose to read books that will further us on this path to awakening. But most importantly, we go back to the yogic practices of seated meditation, movement meditation, breath work, chanting, or the guided relaxations. We allow the practice to do what it does best, to open us up automatically to the knowledge and truth of who and what we really are, opening us up to guidance from our higher self.

Ego as the Major Mind Trick

Asmita is ego, the identification with the false self. Once we have forgotten the truth of who and what we really are (*avidya*), then we easily begin to identify ourselves with this ego-self we create and learn from others. You can also see how the ego (*asmita*) can immerse us so deeply within it that we totally forget the truth of who we are and what's going on (*avidya*). Again, these afflictions seem to perpetuate each other. Once we have established and identified ourselves with the ego, this thought system then perpetuates all the other afflictions of the mind.

If you are identifying with the false self or ego (*asmita*), then you feel limited to the body and so you are scared (*abhinivesah*) that when the body dies, you might die too. This identification with the false self or ego (*asmita*) and ignorance of what's really going on (*avidya*) makes it scary to think about death and to look at the present moment. You may delude (*moha*) yourself out of the present moment with drink, drugs, or overeating because of a deep-seated fear driven by the ego and ignorance that what is there can possibly hurt you. The ego or false self (*asmita*) drives us to avoid (*dvesha*) and desire (*raga*) things that it tricks us into thinking will make us happy and keep us out of pain. So you can see how ego (*asmita)* and ignorance (*avidya)* perpetuate the other afflictions of the mind. This identification with the false self and ignorance really seem to go hand in hand.

Cultivate Remembering Your True Nature

Here we are getting to the root of the problem, and this is where the guided relaxations really come through for us. When we can get to a point in which we can really relax, what does this tell us? It tells us that we are comfortable releasing control. We are comfortable letting go for a moment. When we go into these guided relaxations (savasana as we have talked about in a previous chapter), we momentarily let go of our false ego-self completely as we drop through the body and through the mind into an experience of our true nature. This is so easy! It is so easy that the ego convinces us that simply relaxing has nothing to do with awakening. According to the ego, we must be *doing* something!

The more we practice relaxing, the sooner we find ourselves awake to the truth of who we really are. We come out of deep relaxation feeling renewed, connected, and whole. We take this peaceful feeling into everything we do—that is, until the ego creeps back in and we find ourselves tired, stressed, and anxious again.

Lesson 109 in ACIM workbook is titled, "I Rest in God." The lesson says,

> "I rest in God." This thought will bring to you the rest and quiet, peace and stillness, and the safety and the happiness you seek. "I rest in God." This thought has the power to wake the sleeping truth in you, whose vision sees beyond appearances to that same truth in everyone and everything there is. Here is the end of suffering for all the world, and everyone who ever came and yet will come to linger for a while. Here is the thought in which the Son of God is born again, to recognize himself. (ACIM W-pI.109.2:1–6)

"Rest in Peace" is a common tombstone epitaph. What if we rested in this peace, rested in God, not just in death, but throughout life as well? We would then be living the happy dream!

Attachment as a Major Ego Temptation

Raga is the Sanskrit word for attraction or attachment. "I won't be happy until the weekend. I need a drink, and then I'll be okay. I'll be happy once I get that new car." This is when we are trying to fix our problems on the level of the ego by searching for happiness outside of ourselves. Trying to find happiness from something outside of ourselves is never going to work. Eventually we realize that we are always in that waiting game for happiness. The search is futile until we fully understand that what we are ultimately searching for is the remembrance of our true nature, in which we are *always* home with God.

Dukha is a Sanskrit term that describes the sensation of wanting things but also realizing they don't make you happy. I remind you of what ACIM asks, "What better example could there be of the ego's maxim, "Seek but do not find"?" (ACIM T-16.V.6:5) And this really pertains to *raga* and *dukha*, always seeking but never finding what you are looking for. Another ACIM quote that pertains to *raga:* "And at its [ego] altar, it demands you lay all of the things it bids you get, leaving you no joy in them" (ACIM T-13.VII.10:13). The ego is driving us to want things, but as soon as we get them, there is no lasting joy.

This is a huge temptation and one that can show up in the simplest or most complex ways. It can be as simple as always desiring new material objects or as complex as wanting to feel good enough in a parent's eyes. The ego will drive us to want and desire on many levels, leaving us feeling exhausted, lost, and empty.

Cultivate Non-Attachment

When attachment comes up, we try to cultivate non-attachment. This doesn't mean you have to sell everything you own and walk around in a loincloth with one spiritual book only. You can still have things; it's just about letting go of the *attachment* to those things. You know that if those things were taken from you tomorrow, you would still be perfectly peaceful and happy. It's not going to affect you in your true nature.

In a lot of cases, you may find that you are more attached to the *idea* of needing to get rid of certain things or behaviors in life than to the thing or the behavior itself. This can get tricky, as it's simply the ego trying to send you on another wild goose chase! You always start with remembering your true nature and coming to the realization that whatever it is that you are attached to does not enhance or take away from your true nature. Your true nature is already perfect just the way it is. Once you really get this, everything else will take care of itself in the perfect way in its own time.

My Own Attachment

Working on this book and my website, *ChooseSpiritNow.com*, has made my computer the equivalent of gold to me right now. There is so much work that has gone into this book and the online retreat, and it is all on my laptop. My husband keeps asking me, "Have you backed it up?" A lot of it is backed up, but a lot of it isn't. I keep having this vision and ask myself, "What if someone stole my laptop? Would I be able to stay peaceful?" On one level, I feel all the blood drain out of my body and think, "Oh my goodness, what would I do?" And on another level, I know that if that really happened, then creating this book and program was not for anyone else to see but for me to really get this message of non-attachment. If someone took my computer and I was able to stay peaceful about it, then I would know that I was getting somewhere in terms of living awake. If someone took my computer and I had a heart attack and it took years for me to recover, well, that's fine too. Neither reaction adds to or takes away from my true nature as whole, perfect, and eternal, but why not choose Spirit now, live awake, and enjoy every moment no matter what?

Attachment with Relationships

Another level of this non-attachment or detachment is with our relationships. The ego really comes up for most of us with this one. The knowledge that in our true nature we are all connected in Spirit and absolutely nothing can truly take somebody from us makes ending a relationship a lot easier. If we never get that approval from a parent, we can detach from needing it by realizing our already perfect, eternal nature, and by understanding that our parents' resistance to reaching out to us is their own ego getting in the way. If a loved one passes on, it is a lot easier knowing that this person may have left the body, but they are still connected with us in Spirit. This helps us in our detachment from that person as a body and as the self-image they built in this lifetime. Now we can remember that person as eternal Spirit, whole, perfect, and immortal. Again, we detach not by forcing it but by going to the root of the problem and awakening.

Avoidance as a Major Ego Temptation

Dvesha is avoidance: "I'll be okay as long as I don't have to face my feelings. I will busy myself with a million different things so that I don't have to be still and look inside. Who knows what I will find there?"

We are all guilty of this, and in this day and age, it's easy thanks to the many distractions we have such as phones, computers, and t.v. When we have forgotten our true nature and identify ourselves with the ego, it is pretty easy to avoid what may be happening within us due to the fear of what we may find.

I'm pretty good about connecting and reawakening to my true nature on a daily basis. But every now and then, I'll have a day or so when I get extraordinarily busy in my thinking mind and I don't make time to reconnect. When I finally take a moment to check in, I usually have this welling up of emotion and feeling like, "Ah, I've come back home again."

I notice this happening when I teach after a long Christmas break. I feel like I pick up on that energy in the class. Everyone has been so busy over the holiday and now we are back on our mats, checking in with ourselves, and it's that "Ahhhhhhh!" energy that I feel coming from everyone in the room as we slow down, shift out of ego consciousness, and take the time to remember our truest nature.

Sometimes you may flip-flop back and forth between getting busy and forgetting the bigger picture and then slowing down to remember it again, but when you really know that your true nature is there for you to awaken to in any moment, it makes life a lot easier. It doesn't matter whether you are on a crowded, busy street, on vacation somewhere far away, or in your house vacuuming and doing your daily thing. Every moment is a chance to live *awake*. When life gets busy and distracting, simply the knowledge that we *can* wake up and experience our true nature whenever we want is a good feeling.

> Every moment is a chance to live *awake*. When life gets busy and distracting, simply the knowledge that we *can* wake up and experience our true nature whenever we want is a good feeling.

Avoidance is a powerful ego trick because it can prevent us from looking at and releasing all the other afflictions of the mind. It can sneak up on us without us realizing it. Most importantly, the ego will drive us to avoid looking at it too closely in an effort to save itself. We will avoid awakening because the ego will trick us into thinking that awakening is crazy or not in alignment with our religious beliefs. When looked at closely this is another trick of self-preservation by the ego.

We have discussed that in many traditions, the lower belly is considered the emotional center of the body. For many of us, old emotional wounds have been stored here and we can develop shallow breathing, begin undereating, or overeating in order to no longer access this area of the body. We don't realize that by doing these things, we are avoiding this stored emotion in the belly. We can subsequently experience anxiety, fear, anger, stress, and the inability to digest properly or the inability to feel full when eating. This anxiety, stress, etc. is actually coming from the unconscious avoidance of old stored emotion in the body, due to the fear of it being too painful to face.

My Own Avoidance

When I was young and I was having those first bouts of depression, I remember going to my parents at times and boohooing. They would ask me what was wrong, but I could never pinpoint it. I felt very lonely, but nothing seemed to fill it. The nightly fighting had stopped, but every now and then the memory of my dad's flirtation would be triggered, and my mom would be dragged back through the betrayal all over again. My parents were trying to help me, but they were still in a very raw emotional place themselves. This had been our family secret for so long, and we weren't ready to face the repercussions of what this trying time had had on all of us.

My sister was the only one at the time who could be honest about it. She was the only one who would bring it up in the light of day and curse my mother for what she was doing or my dad for flirting in the first place. I was always appalled. I was scared of rocking the boat. I would rather pretend that it wasn't happening than talk about it and risk it being brought into the daylight as well. I now realize how brave my sister was for willing to be honest about it. She risked upheaval for the sake of bringing it to light. The rest of us were using avoidance to completely brush it under the rug. We thought we were doing ourselves a favor, but in reality, we were just making it worse.

Because of this avoidance, I began dealing with my emotions by overeating. I was a skinny kid, but I could eat until my belly was huge. I never felt full. I realized later that I was using food to cut myself off from these feelings. Disappointment would rise up from overeating again, but at least I didn't have to face these other emotions that were scurrying around inside.

I was also good at *not* eating for periods of time. I would starve myself for periods of time, and then I would binge and eat a ton of food until my belly was huge again. When I was starving myself, it felt like I was holding my breath until I was ready to binge eat again. I never made myself throw up, but the effect was the same. I was controlling myself with food and reinforcing avoidance of these painful emotions.

When I first started practicing yoga and I was sobbing through the poses, I was finally coming face to face with these emotions that had been ruminating and marinating in my body for what felt like ages. It was so strange yet utterly exhilarating at the same time to begin to feel this core part of my body again. As the emotions came up and out, I was able to feel my belly from the inside out without it being emotionally painful. I didn't realize until later that a lot of the anger and frustration that I had been carrying around all those years was from this intense holding back and avoidance of all these other deeply held emotions. Subconsciously, I anticipated them to be too painful to face.

After practicing yoga for a while, I began to feel full when eating, and that was amazing to me. I still overate for a time, because it was such a habit for me at that point, but eventually I was able to release the habit. I notice that I can still overeat at times, but now, I know that I can take the time to slow down and check in with myself to figure out what I am trying to avoid so that I can release it.

I know there are a lot of people out there who are cutting themselves off from this belly area through shallow breathing or overeating in an attempt to avoid this stored emotion and keep stuffing it down further into the belly. Hopefully they will be led to yoga one day and understand the benefits of nonavoidance as they learn to access this storehouse of emotional energy.

Cultivate Nonavoidance

Once we really understand our true nature, we realize that the ugliness of the ego, in all its forms, is not the real us. We can now face anything that we are avoiding without fear or embarrassment.

Yoga practice helps us to cultivate nonavoidance. We learn to deepen the breath. We learn to breathe into that lower belly, into that emotional center that is holding all of this stored emotion. We shine the light on what we are trying to avoid. At first, it is a little scary, but if we keep it up, we begin to access the emotional energy and memory that we have trapped there. As we stay connected to our emotional center through the *ujjayi* breath, this allows us to release and purify these old stored emotions.

Eventually we realize that a good part of our day is spent busying ourselves so much so that we don't have time to experience this trapped emotion. But if we take the time to slow down and face it, we find that what is there isn't scary at all. If we can stay with it and breathe through it, the healing naturally takes place. The veil to peace is lifted. The next time you notice yourself getting uncomfortable and holding your breath or overeating, try to take a nice, deep breath. See if that is enough to let that discomfort go. If not, take another deep breath, and another, until this discomfort has been exhaled from the body. If this is not enough, try a movement meditation practice coupled with breath work.

The bottom line is to *choose Spirit now* and remember your true nature as whole, perfect, and eternal. Know that this avoidance does nothing to take away from that; it only takes away from your *remembrance* of that. The process and practice is necessary only because you are not believing in or remembering your true nature in every moment as of yet. Don't fret! It will happen! Until it does, keep up with the self-study and practices.

Delusion as a Major Ego Temptation

Moha is delusion. "I'll drink, do drugs, or eat too much to totally delude myself out of what's in front of me." Maybe the present moment is too painful or too scary or too seemingly boring, so we just delude ourselves out of it completely. Delusion is an extreme form of avoidance. As long as we are deluding ourselves out of the present moment, we will most likely not be able to release the ego or experience ourselves in our true nature as Spirit. It's still possible, but it's like covering yourself with soundproof material to deafen yourself even more against the guidance from Holy Spirit.

Nouk Sanchez and Tomas Vieira have a wonderful CD collection called *The Miracle of Trust: Overcoming the One Obstacle to Love's Infinite Presence.* In it, they say a mental breakdown is the beginning of a spiritual breakthrough. This is great news! A lot of us have been to that point in life where we felt close to a mental breakdown. But we do everything in our power not to break down, not to admit to these emotions because of the stigma attached as weakness or craziness. We stuff our emotions down in our bodies, put on a good face, and walk through life like a ticking time bomb, settling our "nerves" with alcohol, drugs, food, whatever. If we can attach new meaning to a mental breakdown as Nouk and Tomas describe it (as a potential spiritual breakthrough), then we are getting somewhere. We come to understand that we *can* face these emotions knowing they have absolutely no effect on who and what we are as our true nature.

> We stuff our emotions down in our bodies, put on a good face, and walk through life like a ticking time bomb, settling our "nerves" with alcohol, drugs, food, whatever.

It usually takes getting pushed to the limit, feeling backed into a corner, maybe even wanting to end our lives, to finally wake up and realize that there has to be a better way and that something is really wrong. *There is a better way,* and it is really simple. *Choose Spirit now* and choose to remember your true nature in Spirit (created in God's image) as whole, perfect, and eternal.

Cultivate Staying Present

The opposite of delusion is staying present. Anything you can do or love to do that brings you into the present moment, *do it!* Practice yoga, pick up an old hobby, or go for a walk on the beach *without* thinking and analyzing your way through the sand. Make time for things in

137

your daily life that you know bring you out of your habitual patterns of thinking and analyzing and bring you back to the present moment.

Being present allows you to experience your true nature as whole, perfect, and eternal. When you tap into this, then you can allow yourself to break down in a safe space realizing that there is no point in continuing to delude yourself out of facing aspects of your false ego-self. As a matter of fact, facing these aspects of the false self—no matter how scary they seem to be— will allow them to burn up and disappear. The ego tricks you into thinking that facing these aspects of your false self will be too painful, too embarrassing, and too much for you to handle. But in reality, the ability to stop the delusion and come into the present *is your invitation* to finally release all of the fear and experience your true nature as unconditional love, deep peace, and abundant joy. Ask yourself if whatever you are doing is worth deluding yourself out of what could potentially be a spiritual breakthrough.

The ego tricks you into thinking that facing these aspects of your false self will be too painful, too embarrassing, and too much for you to handle. But in reality, the ability to stop the delusion and come into the present *is your invitation* to finally release all of the fear and experience your true nature as unconditional love, deep peace, and abundant joy.

Good High vs. Bad High

When we drink or use drugs, we get a high, but when we come down, we come down lower than where we started. We come down lower than normal. That low is the hangover, the guilt, and the blues or even depression that ensues from a night of binge drinking or a night of snorting cocaine. When we practice yoga, get a massage, or play with a hobby we love, we can also experience a high. The difference is you come back down to normal. You don't go lower than normal and experience a hangover.

Release Stored Emotional Energy that Is Driving Your Addiction

When you use addictions to delude yourself out of the present moment because there is stored emotional energy that you fear is too painful to face, restrain yourself from using them; allow some of this emotional energy to come up so that you can release it. Withhold that object of addiction and allow the feelings of withdrawal to surface. Take this time to breathe into that lower belly and allow any feelings of anger and frustration to come up. Keep breathing and see if you can find other emotions hiding behind that anger and frustration. Allow yourself to fully experience these emotions; cry or get upset. *Be* what you are feeling in this moment. Be at peace with it. This releases the stored emotional energy that drives the addiction. Have you ever noticed how calm and peaceful you feel after facing these pent-up emotions and releasing them through a good cry? If you continue working to free this emotional energy, eventually there will be nothing to hide from and no addiction necessary.

Remember that it is *your choice* to continue with your addiction or let it go. Addiction does nothing to lessen your true nature, *but it does prevent you from remembering it.* When you are ready, you *will choose to remember* because that is the only thing your higher self truly wants for you. Sometimes the ego has you so tied into thinking you need this addiction that it takes an outside-in approach, in this case some sort of rehab program, which enables you to get sober enough to begin seeing the light.

My Experience with Delusion

When I began massage school at age twenty-two, I felt as if my world of gray was finally being splashed again with color. This was fourteen years after the childhood drama began, fourteen years of on-and-off depression in a gray and lonely world.

I had a teacher in massage school who taught a class called Body/Mind/Spirit Integration, and I loved it. She taught us creative exercises to really dig deep to find trapped emotional energy to release. We used creative journaling to access the inner child. When I started seeing my teacher for counseling after school, she recommended specific self-help books and tapes which really brought the light of awareness to what had been going on inside of me all these years.

I felt like I had finally found what I was looking for. Life started feeling meaningful again. The problem was, it didn't last very long. The light inside me was like a light switch, turning on and off. There would be days that I would wake up and life was beautiful. The next day, I couldn't even get out of bed.

At this time, I was drinking heavily on the weekends and sometimes even dabbling with drugs. I didn't drink during the week, but the weekends were two nights of being obliterated from alcohol and/or drugs and two days of being exhausted, hung over, and depressed. In hindsight, I realized that during the week, I was taking two steps forward with my self-help exercises, but on the weekends, I was taking three steps back with the drinking and the drugs.

It took a five-night binge on cocaine to finally make me quit drugs for good a few years later at twenty-five. I'll never forget calling my sister and telling her that I couldn't remember ever having a good reason for wanting to get out of bed, much less making the bed afterward. I remember her telling me that I had to stop doing this to myself. I didn't know if I could really do it at the time, but I vowed I would never take drugs again. With the help of nothing less than God and my higher self, I almost kept my promise.

Less than a year later, at twenty-six, I had one last night on ecstasy and cocaine. The experience sealed the deal for me. I was finally clear enough at that point to realize that the guilt and depression I suffered after a drug binge was just not worth it. I also had been letting go little by little of that false self-image of being one of the "cool girls" who did drugs with the guys. I began to understand that there was a higher part of myself that had always been trying to guide me. Now, I finally trusted that part of myself to guide me in the right direction, and, at that point, away from anything that may tempt me to make bad choices again.

I still drank heavily on some weekends, but over the years, as I released more and more of my false self-image and insecurity, my drinking decreased. When I remarried at thirty-one, I didn't drink that often, but when I did, I still drank to excess and felt horrible the next day. Once we had our little girl, Rowen, when I was thirty-two, the hangovers weren't worth the drinks. Finally, at age thirty-five, I gave up alcohol completely.

Once I quit drinking, it became even more clear how negatively the alcohol was affecting my life, especially emotionally. This was now thirteen years after I had been first introduced to yoga in massage school. My practice deepened and evolved over the years, and I know it was this yoga practice that brought me to the realization of my true nature and enabled me eventually to let these bad habits go.

Right before I quit drinking for good, I had a girls' weekend at the beach with my friends. After the weekend, it took me until the next Thursday to begin feeling normal again. I was down and depressed and tired. It was a wake-up call for me. I was finally at a point in my life where I felt really good until I drank. I didn't like things getting me down anymore. Even the anticipation of drinking, knowing that I would be hung over the next day, was uncomfortable. I no longer needed or wanted the things that were dragging me down—alcohol and cigarettes. I quit for good the following month.

Getting Honest with Ourselves

If you have some problems with drinking or drugs, hopefully you can eventually let that go. This is a good place to really get honest with yourself. When you drink or pop a pill, you are taking yourself out of the present. Look at that and ask yourself, "What am I trying to avoid here? What am I trying to delude myself out of?" Pick up that flashlight and start shining the light to see what's going on inside that you are trying to avoid. If you can face it and start releasing it, eventually you will find that you need that drink or that drug less and less.

Fear of Death as a Major Ego Trick

Abhinivesah, the fear of death, is instinctual. "I'm so fearful of death that I will think of everything that could possibly happen to me so that I can prevent it. I limit my activities in life because of the fear that they may bring me death." This is one of the ego's biggest manipulators. There are a lot of us living life with this fear hanging over our heads, and it's preventing us from living fully. How do we let go of this fear? Through more experiences of our true nature in Spirit.

Fear of death *(abhinivesah)* was an affliction I had definitely come to know. As a child, I remember having horrid images of a wrecking ball crashing into my house and my family dead and gone. I was petrified of something happening to my family, and the fear was sometimes paralyzing.

Cultivate Remembering Your True Nature as Eternal

Savasana is corpse pose/relaxation pose. This pose was designed to not only take us into deep relaxation but to help us face our fear of death. In *savasana*, we go into such a deep state of relaxation that we drop through the body, through the mind, and we find ourselves pretty quickly experiencing this state of Spirit in which we feel infinite and connected to every aspect of creation. We have full knowledge of our eternal nature. With this knowledge, there is no fear of death.

When we see ourselves through the lens of the ego, we see ourselves as limited to this body, which ends in death. When we see ourselves from our true nature, we recognize ourselves as eternal Spirit created by God in His image, with no death to fear.

Many of us fear death, but we also fear *how* we are going to die. Is it going to be some long, drawn-out, torturous process, or is it going to be so quick that we don't even know that we died? We will be walking around as a ghost, wondering why everyone's ignoring us. Through our experience of death, we can still use these processes to experience death fully, to stay present and see the *beauty* in our death, even as we pass out of this body. It doesn't mean we won't fight for our lives since that is deeply instinctual. But within the fight, we can still connect with our higher self and experience the beauty of our passing.

It is normal for parents to worry about their children passing before them. This fear is hard to face. Once you do, it can bring lasting peace and allow you to let go enough to fully enjoy life with your child without that fear hanging over your head all the time. I sometimes imagine if Rowen were to pass from this life before me. I know I would experience immense sorrow at the loss of feeling her arms around me, hearing her voice, or the sheer joy it brings me in just having her near. I know I would have to allow myself to experience the grief fully. But I also know I have awakened enough to know that in truth, she is always with me. If I am able to experience the grief fully and release it as it comes, I will have moments of clarity. I will have moments of full knowledge of our connection, of our Oneness. I know that there would be moments of wanting to take my own life in the utmost form of avoidance of the sorrow and of the grief that comes with the loss of a child. But the bottom line is, whether I made it through her death or ended up taking my own life, either way doesn't take away from my true nature as perfect, whole, and eternal and the reality that I am always and forever connected with Rowen, no matter what. I can only hope that I would be able to get to that remembrance, that awakening, without taking my own life and then be able to share my experience with people going through similar situations.

Ana Forrest, in her book *Fierce Medicine,* has a wonderful death meditation journaling exercise that is a great way to face your impending death and release the fear you may have surrounding it. In facing death we are able to figure out what matters most to us in life which enables us to then enjoy these things while we are still having this experience in the body.

A friend of mine and her sister put together a website called *mymemorialcelebration.com.* It's a way for you to plan your memorial. It's also a great way to face your impending death and see it as a celebration. This may make it easier for your loved ones as they realize that you weren't fearful of your own death and saw it as something to be celebrated.

Summary

All of these ego tricks or afflictions of the mind lead to the feelings of dissatisfaction, pain and suffering, unhappiness and unfulfillment, fear and stress. Sound familiar? It's like a house of mirrors. Each of the afflictions really helps to perpetuate each other and keep us in this cycle of pain and suffering. These afflictions of the mind are truly fascinating. What's more fascinating to me is that, more than four thousand years ago, they were written about in the Vedas—and are still just as relevant today.

Why do we need self-study, discipline, practice, and guidance from Holy Spirit?

In *The Wisdom of Yoga*, Stephen Cope says that moments of freedom from our habitual patterns "bring glimpses of Illumined Mind. But these awakenings are fragile. They collapse under the tremendous power of the self-representation—I, Me, and Mine—and the chain of longing, clinging, craving, and *dukha* begins all over again" (Cope 2006, 137).

We all have these moments of awakening, but in an instant, the ego can pull us back down into its grip. "The power of affliction, of *raga*, and *dvesha*, is so great that when combined with *asmita*, *samskara*, and *vasana*, it simply cannot be deconstructed by the unaided human will" (Cope 2006, 137). In other words, the ego is extremely manipulative and it cannot be undone by what Cope calls the *unaided human will*. We need all the help we can get from the Holy Spirit, our higher self, to keep leading us back out of the darkness and into the light of truth.

My Ego Tricks and Temptations

As I continue to find myself pulled into the ego's grip, I find that the most important lesson is to forgive myself for allowing it to happen. I am also reminded to have compassion for others when ego takes over them too. Every time I get pulled back down by the ego, I find there is a silver lining, another gift from my higher self urging me to live awake and to be another beacon of light. No pressure, of course!

In the next chapter we will learn the *biggest ego temptation* that, even when understood, can manipulate us into *staying immersed* in the ego cloud. We will also learn the *biggest ego trick* that is so well constructed that even the most spiritual of teachers can fall into its trap.

CHAPTER 17

Spiritualizing the Ego (the Ego's Biggest Trick) & Step 4 to Awakening

We don't turn away from our story until we realize that our story isn't going anywhere.
—Tom Carpenter *A Dialogue on Forgiveness*
DVD (Carpenter and Holden, 2010)

Specialness as a Huge Ego Temptation

What happens when there are aspects of the ego that we don't want to let go of? Once we have built this false self-image, we become attached to this striving for specialness and perfection. This desire for specialness and perfection falls under the ego temptation (*klesha*) of attachment or attraction (*raga*) that we discussed in the last chapter. This ego temptation also drives another ego trick, avoidance, because we want to avoid anything that threatens this "specialness."

Yearning for specialness is one of the ego's biggest temptations in life and therefore one of the biggest ego hurdles to overcome. Most of us want to please somebody in our lives and make them proud. We want to be *special* in their eyes. The problem is, we usually do this at the cost of trying to

> Yearning for specialness is one of the ego's biggest temptations in life and therefore one of the biggest ego hurdles to overcome.

be *better* and *more special* than someone else. This ego temptation of specialness is difficult to overcome. We will continue to put up a good fight for specialness because in our ego-self, we don't want to be *equal*. We want to be *special*.

What you are in your true nature is the most perfect love, peace, and joy you can ever imagine. What the *ego* doesn't like to hear is, *so is everyone else*. ACIM says, "You would oppose this course because it teaches you, you and your brother are alike" (ACIM T-24.I.8:6). It also says, "Unless you think that all your brothers have an equal right to miracles with you, you will not claim your right to them because you were unjust to one with equal rights. Seek to deny and you will feel denied. Seek to deprive, and you have been deprived" (ACIM T-25.IX.8:1-3).

> As long as we desire to be better than others, we will be at the mercy of the ego.

As long as we desire to be better than others, we will be at the mercy of the ego. This is a tough one.

Ego's Highs and Lows

Imagine you are flying high on a big promotion and feeling like a bigwig at the office. This high is super-enjoyable. You are feeling confident, cocky, and indestructible. Out of the blue, a close friend passes away, and suddenly, your high on that promotion seems pale and ridiculous in comparison to the death of your friend. You tell yourself you're a fake and a phony and ridiculous for even thinking your life was great when you received that promotion. You even ask yourself, "How could you have ever thought you were worthwhile at all? You're not even worth the job you had right out of college."

You find yourself down in the dumps with loser thoughts and subsequent feelings of guilt, fear, and inadequacy. The ego is that voice in your head building you up to make you feel better and more special than others. But rest assured, at some point it will be tearing you down, making you feel like a worthless sack of poo. (Yes, I said "poo.")

When you seem to be on top in life, and feeling "special" according to the ego's definition, you might be having a lot of fun, but the joke is on you. When you enjoy the ego's high on "specialness," at some point, you will have to experience the ego's low. Maybe that specialness gets taken from you, or maybe something else happens in life that makes your specialness suddenly seem mediocre or worthless.

When this happens, we continue to drive ourselves with this desire for specialness in order to prove ourselves worthy and seek out that ego high once again. It's addictive to feel special. That's why this is such a big ego hurtle. That's why it is so important to begin that process of

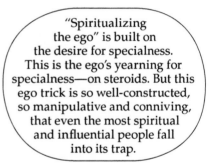

When this happens, we continue to drive ourselves with this desire for specialness in order to prove ourselves worthy and seek out that ego high once again. It's addictive to feel special.

detaching from the ego. Until you detach to a certain degree, you won't be able to even begin to let go of this yearning, this desire for specialness.

Spiritualizing the Ego

"Spiritualizing the ego" is built on the desire for specialness. This is the ego's yearning for specialness—on steroids. But this ego trick is so well-constructed, so manipulative and conniving, that even the most spiritual and influential people fall into its trap.

"Spiritualizing the ego" is built on the desire for specialness. This is the ego's yearning for specialness—on steroids. But this ego trick is so well-constructed, so manipulative and conniving, that even the most spiritual and influential people fall into its trap.

It hides beneath good intentions, but it is still the ego making you think you are better than others, more worthy than others, more knowledgeable than others. Ego can show up in the most holy of spiritual people. No one is immune.

You can see priests living from Spirit—and priests living from ego. You can see gurus living from Spirit—and gurus living from ego. You can see people giving to charity from a place of Spirit—or from a place of ego. When you are around these people, you can feel it in a heartbeat if the ego is in control. This is not a time for judgment. Instead, notice how easily the ego can trick anyone with its manipulations. Now is the time for self-study and reflection. Has the ego fooled you into "spiritualizing the ego"? Don't be afraid. It happens to the best of us. *The first and most difficult step is to be able to admit to it.*

If you have ever noticed a part of you that feels more worthy than others, more spiritual than others, like you are further on the path than others then this is the ego's trick once again. Your desire for specialness is driving you to avoid the truth that we were *all* created in perfection as *One* in Spirit in God's image; no ifs, ands, or buts.

I was guilty of spiritualizing the ego. When I first started practicing yoga, I was releasing a lot of my ego, but on some level, I was building more ego because I was still comparing myself to others. But now it was about "I'm more peaceful than her." When a friend called to unload, I would think, *I'm so glad I don't have to deal with these kinds of problems anymore,* as I judged them in my head.

I would always recommend yoga to people, because I knew how transformational it was for me, but to be honest, there was always a part of me (the ego part) that really didn't want them to do yoga. I didn't want them to be as peaceful as me. How crazy is that? The Course says, "It will be given you to see your brother's worth when all you want for him is peace. And what you want for him you will receive." (ACIM T-20.V.3:6-7) We cannot allow the ego to take the reins and desire specialness and perfection for only ourselves. We must eventually realize we are all in this together and we must desire peace and perfection for each other as well, in order to truly experience it within ourselves. Sometimes the ego is so involved that we have a tough time wanting to share this with others. The Course really helps drive home the point that it is in our desire for peace and awakening for *all* of our brothers and sisters that we are truly able to awaken ourselves. And we *will* be able to do this with the help of Holy Spirit.

I remember a particular day at my dad's house. We were having a conversation in the front yard as I was about to get in my car to leave. Dad said something that I will never forget. "Ginger," he said, "just be sure you aren't spiritualizing the ego." Now I had never heard this term before, but I knew exactly what it meant. And without hesitation, I replied, "Oh no, of course not. I wouldn't do that." As I got in my car and drove off, I knew *immediately* that was *exactly* what I was doing.

Talk about avoidance. I did not want to face that one! It was embarrassing, but I knew I had to face it or risk being called out on it again by my dad. Even when I first began teaching yoga, there was a healthy level of ego to my teaching, but as soon as I realized what was happening, I was careful to watch it. Now when I feel that ego arise, most of the time I can pretty easily let it go.

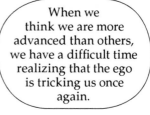

As silly as this sounds, I really had to look my ego in the eye and say, "I'm not better than somebody else because I'm more peaceful. I'm not better than somebody else because I do yoga every day." When we think we are more advanced than others, we have a difficult time realizing that the ego is tricking us once again.

> When we think we are more advanced than others, we have a difficult time realizing that the ego is tricking us once again.

Remember, ego can show up anywhere. It can show up in people with the best intentions. It can show up in the best yoga teachers and gurus and in the most sacred of ashrams or yoga centers. The ego has to be pretty powerful to pull the wool over the eyes of priests, gurus, and spiritual teachers. A lot of times, these teachers are still doing a lot of good, but at the same time, they are building their own ego rather than releasing it—and that's the difference.

As spiritual teachers (gurus, priests, yoga teachers, therapists), we should be asking ourselves every day whether or not we are spiritualizing the ego. Believe me, you will know immediately by the desire to avoid this question altogether or the shameful feeling that will pop up out of nowhere! *This is no place for us to judge.* It's a chance to notice how manipulative the ego is and continue working on our own. Allow compassion to fill your heart for yourself and others as you see the ego at work struggling for its own self-preservation.

> As spiritual teachers (gurus, priests, yoga teachers, therapists), we should be asking ourselves every day whether or not we are spiritualizing the ego.

Why We Are Not All Awakened

Sure, awakening to the truth that we are all equal and One in total perfection, created in God's image, sounds great. But the truth is, while we are immersed in this ego thought system, we don't want to be equal. We want to be special!

> But the truth is, while we are immersed in this ego thought system, we don't want to be equal. We want to be special!

We will continue to want to be special until we finally realize that the lows are not worth the highs and we want something different for ourselves. Again, as long as we desire to be better than others, we are at the mercy of the ego. "I want to be special," is an aspect of that ego mind temptation of attachment and attraction. It will continue to tempt us until we awaken to realize that *in reality* (our true nature) we *can never be* more special than another. In Oneness *there is no "other"*.

> It will continue to tempt us until we awaken to realize that *in reality* (our true nature) we *can never be* more special than another. In Oneness *there is no "other"*.

Tom Carpenter says in his conversation with Robert Holden, PhD in the excellent DVD, *A Dialogue on Forgiveness*, "We don't turn away from our story until we realize that our story isn't going anywhere" (Carpenter and Holden, 2010). We don't let go of that desire for specialness or quit clinging onto our false self-image until we finally realize that it *cannot* get us anywhere. Our misidentification with the ego *cannot* fill us with true happiness and fulfillment. The ego just keeps sending us on wild goose chase after wild goose chase, causing us to feel less joyful and less fulfilled as we can *never* catch up to what we are truly searching for.

> We don't let go of that desire for specialness or quit clinging onto our false self-image until we finally realize that it *cannot* get us anywhere. Our misidentification with the ego *cannot* fill us with true happiness and fulfillment.

Abusive Relationship Analogy

This is another reason why we have a difficult time waking up from the ego. We are so entrenched in its belief system in our lives that we are comfortable with it, despite all the misery it causes us. Just as in an abusive relationship, people tend to stay because it is what they know, it is what they are familiar with. It seems easier to stay in an abusive relationship rather than risk the discomfort of trying to leave and find a new relationship. Even though our true nature is

> Even though our true nature is the most peaceful, wonderful, and perfect state of our own reality, the ego has tricked us into choosing its world over the happy dream that is here for us in every moment. It has tricked us into staying in this illusion.

150

the most peaceful, wonderful, and perfect state of our own reality, the ego has tricked us into choosing its world over the happy dream that is here for us in every moment. It has tricked us into staying in this illusion.

One partner in an abusive relationship runs down the other partner and tells them, "You'll never find someone else who loves you like I love you. That's why I treat you this way." That is the ego working in that person, but it is also analogous to the ego working in our own lives. The ego tricks us and scares us into thinking certain ways and feeling certain ways. Just as when someone manipulates their partner into staying in an abusive relationship, ego manipulates us into staying in its made-up mental construct.

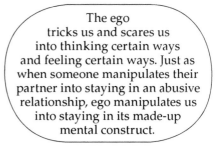

The ego tricks us and scares us into thinking certain ways and feeling certain ways. Just as when someone manipulates their partner into staying in an abusive relationship, ego manipulates us into staying in its made-up mental construct.

How to Overcome This Ego Hurtle of Specialness

We have to shine the light on the areas in our life in which this desire for specialness is showing up. We have to ask ourselves, "Is it worth it?" We have to understand that when we choose to hold on to our inequality and our specialness, we are preventing ourselves from experiencing effortless guidance through life. We are preventing ourselves from experiencing unlimited creative potential and connection with others. We are preventing ourselves from experiencing the wonder of living in harmony with creation. The ego will continue to try and trick you into thinking that you can still hold on to parts of the ego that you like while you are letting go of others. As long as you are enjoying the ego's highs, you can bet that soon enough you will have to suffer the ego's lows.

A combination of what the Course calls that "little willingness" to be open to Holy Spirit's guidance, and the yoga practice which will facilitate your opening back up to Holy Spirit's guidance, will allow you to move past this ego hurtle and awaken. Now you will experience unlimited creativity, connection and the feeling as if you are living in harmony with creation. These experiences give incentive to continue moving you forward on this path, choosing to remember your true nature in every moment rather than be tempted by the ego's desire for specialness which only leads to separation, competition, and loneliness.

Remember, judgment is the backbone of this ego mental construct. As you make mistakes throughout this process and feel judgment arise, notice it and immediately let it go. This ensures that even through the mistake of choosing ego over Spirit, choosing specialness over Oneness, you are still dismantling the ego by letting judgment over your "wrong" choice go.

If you find yourself choosing the ego's specialness and separation over Spirit's Oneness and inclusion, forgive yourself. Don't judge yourself and feel guilty. Remember, judgment is the backbone of this ego mental construct. As you make mistakes throughout this process and feel judgment arise, notice it and immediately let it go. This ensures that even through the mistake of choosing ego over Spirit, choosing specialness over Oneness, you are still dismantling the ego by letting judgment over your "wrong" choice go.

It's all about nonjudgmental observation as you move along this path, eventually realizing that there is no path. There is only the now, which extends for eternity and the ability to live awake in this eternal moment.

It's all about nonjudgmental observation as you move along this path, eventually realizing that there is no path. There is only the now, which extends for eternity and the ability to live awake in this eternal moment.

Shrinking Our Self-Image for Others

Once we begin to shed the ego and find ourselves living spiritually fulfilled lives, we may have times in which we shrink our self-images for the benefit of others. This is another ego trap for you to fall into.

For instance, if you are beginning to live the happy dream and someone comes along whose life isn't so easy, then you may find yourself building a false self-image for them. You show them a self-image that doesn't look so good, in an attempt to make them feel better about their own situation. This is another ego trick. You are actually judging their life experience rather than seeing through the ego. This is when you need to remember to simply stay true to what you are experiencing in your awakening. Shrinking yourself down into a false self-image to make your friend feel better does nothing to lead them to the light. In actuality it strengthens the ego mental construct for both of you and prevents you from remembering that no situation, however bad it may seem, can take away from their true nature as whole, perfect, and eternal.

Some of us have simply gotten into a bad habit of talking about how hard our lives are. We get to the point of competing with friends in this regard. The ego loves competition so much, it even enjoys competing for whose life sucks the worst! "You think that's bad? Listen to what happened to me today!" Sound familiar?

We need to get out of this bad habit with friends. Maybe we fear appearing boastful, but if we are coming from the remembrance of our true nature, then we will not appear boastful because the ego is not involved. As you stand strong in your awakened state, your friends who seem to be struggling will be drawn to your light. So now, if your friend calls you up and says, "Hey, listen to how bad my life sucks," you hold back from wanting to shrink yourself for them. Instead, simply *listen* and *withhold judgment*.

Ask for guidance as you remember the truth that you are one with them in Spirit: whole, perfect, and eternal. On a level that we cannot understand completely, this will positively affect you both astronomically by lifting you both out of this ego mental construct. So give that gift to yourself and your friends. We will talk more in depth about this as truth holding in a later chapter.

I want to share a passage from Marianne Williamson's excellent book, *A Return to Love: Reflections on the Principles of A Course in Miracles*.

> Our deepest fear is not that we are inadequate. Our deepest fear is that we are powerful beyond measure. It is our light, not our darkness that most frightens us. We ask ourselves, Who am I to be brilliant, gorgeous, talented, fabulous? Actually, who are you not to be? You are a child of God. Your playing small does not serve the world. There is nothing enlightened about shrinking so that other people won't feel insecure around you. We are all meant to shine, as children

do. We were born to make manifest the glory of God that is within us. It's not just in some of us; it's in everyone. And as we let our own light shine, we unconsciously give other people permission to do the same. As we are liberated from our own fear, our presence automatically liberates others. (Williamson 1992, 190–191)

Don't be afraid to let your light shine. Don't be afraid to show others what is possible.

Step 4 to Awakening: Recognize the Desire for Specialness and Avoidance of Anything that Threatens this Specialness

Because this is such a powerful ego temptation to overcome, I have an entire step to awakening built upon this one. Shining the light on this area is crucial to the ability to further yourself on the path to awakening. As you recognize this temptation and ask Holy Spirit's help to release it, you are once again naturally detaching from the ego, Step 3 to awakening.

As we move through Step 3 and begin to detach from the ego, we more easily recognize our desire for specialness and can learn to face anything that we are avoiding that threatens this specialness. These steps, 3 and 4, rely on each other for progression out of the ego mind-set.

It takes careful self-study to discriminate between living the happy dream and living a life of specialness and avoidance with the ego pulling the strings. A good way to determine if ego or Spirit is guiding you is to ask yourself if your feelings of joy are inclusive or exclusive. If there is a desire to show off your life in any way or rub your joy in someone's face, ego is at the helm. Remember, *simply being able to recognize this is a huge step in detachment*. The ego won't let go of its grip on specialness very easily. Ask for Holy Spirit's help, and you *will* be guided from within.

In the next chapter, get ready to dive into relationships and how they reveal even more of this ego cloud so that we can continue releasing it.

CHAPTER 18

Relationships Serve as Mirrors & Step 5 to Awakening

> As long as I live, I will never see the center of my own back. Only through mirroring, through the process of reflection—I have to rely on reflection to see these parts. Likewise, there are aspects of my own psyche, my soul even, that I will never ever be able to see by myself. They must be seen and reflected back to me, both my potentials and my embedded dysfunctions. I'll need a human mirror to see those.
>
> —Stephen Cope, *Four Functions of the Transformation Teacher* CD (Cope 2004)

I want to give you a heads-up: some of what we will be talking about in these next three chapters will undoubtedly bring up some ego resistance. I want to remind you that this is what the self-study of yoga is all about. Through the self-study, we are shining the light on every nook and cranny, to see where the ego is hiding out. Through the self-study, we are continuously asking ourselves if we are still holding on to this old ego thought and belief system that is no longer serving us.

Remember, you now have the tools and the process from yoga and ACIM to allow this resistance to come up and then release it. So as we move through these chapters, use the process to stay present and allow the light of self-study to shine through. Observe yourself and whatever thoughts and feelings come up as we move through the next few chapters of information, making sure the ego does not tempt you with avoidance and judgment for its own self-preservation.

Relationships Serve as Mirrors for How We See Ourselves

Relationships can show us a lot. They can show us whether we are living from Spirit or ego, living the happy dream or in the illusion, and they can also show us which ego tricks and temptations are at play to keep us under the ego's spell. Initially we look at all of our relationships with other people: family, friends, and strangers. If we are seeing ourselves as One and connected with all of creation through our true nature as Spirit, then our relationships with others will reflect peace and harmony. If we are seeing ourselves through the lens of the ego as a body and self-image that we have to build and protect, then our relationships with others will reflect discomfort and disharmony.

As difficult as this is to comprehend sometimes, discomfort and disharmony in relationships serve the purpose of showing us that our ego's specialness is under threat from another. Be sure that once this happens, all the ego's tricks and temptations come out full force. Stephen Cope said it best when he describes the process of mirroring in relationship. Relationships bring our deep-seated fears stemming from the ego's thought system to the surface so that we can either take a good look at them and start releasing them—or turn the other cheek and use our ego tricks and temptations to stuff them all back down and move on in various states of suffering.

Relationships bring our deep-seated fears stemming from the ego's thought system to the surface so that we can either take a good look at them and start releasing them—or turn the other cheek and use our ego tricks and temptations to stuff them all back down and move on in various states of suffering.

Let's look at some examples of this discomfort and disharmony showing up in different relationships. If a stranger cuts you off in traffic and this brings up anger and hatred in the form of road rage, this is your clue that ego is in control. If a family member or friend does something that you react to with defensive behavior (or behavior in the form of a retaliatory attack), this is another clue that you are working from ego rather than being guided from Spirit. Even the relationship with yourself is a telltale sign of how much you are living with ego in control. Listen to what goes on in your mind; if you hear a lot of negativity and judgment toward yourself or others as you compare yourself to them, then you know there is even more ego for you to work on seeing through and undoing.

When we feel discomfort and disharmony in our relationships, we can be willing to bet that we are using avoidance techniques to avoid anything we feel might threaten our ego's specialness. When we utilize the yogic self-study to look more closely, we find that the emotions of guilt, fear, jealousy, and insecurity are what threaten our specialness. These are the underlying emotions we are trying to avoid because facing them and admitting to them would be admitting that we do not feel perfect or special, which is utter failure from an ego standpoint. This avoidance is what then causes the discomfort and disharmony in the relationship.

No one likes to admit to feeling guilty, jealous, or insecure because of the threat to the ego self-image. It's equivalent to admitting that we are not special and are weak and fearful (in other words...we suck). However, if we can remember that these emotions have no affect on us in our true nature which is already whole, perfect, and eternal, then we can look at these feelings head-on and realize they have no real power over us (in other words...who cares if we suck in our false-self, that's pretty much its mo anyway). When we identify with our true nature, these emotions can no longer signify weakness in us if we are no longer working from the ego-self (in other words...we *cannot* suck in our true nature). When we understand projection in relationships, we can use this projection as a reminder to face and release any conscious and unconscious stored emotional energy, dismantling this ego mental construct for good.

No one likes to admit to feeling guilty, jealous, or insecure because of the threat to the ego self-image. It's equivalent to admitting that we are not special and are weak and fearful (in other words...we suck). However, if we can remember that these emotions have no affect on us in our true nature which is already whole, perfect, and eternal, then we can look at these feelings head-on and realize they have no real power over us (in other words...who cares if we suck in our false-self, that's pretty much its mo anyway).

Projection

When we identify falsely with our body and self-image, we believe we are separate and unequal. As a result, we continually strive to be "better" than others, something we talked about in the last chapter. We fear death or damage to our self-image and are constantly comparing ourselves to others. Whether we feel that we don't measure up to someone or we feel we are superior to them, we project our deep-seated fear, guilt, jealousy, and insecurities onto them by judging and finding fault with them. This is our last-ditch effort to make *our* self-image look better (and by extension, make ourselves *feel* better) by making others look worse.

ACIM says, "Wisdom is not judgment; it is the relinquishment of judgment" (ACIM M-10.4:5). It also says, "Therefore lay judgment down, not with regret but with a sigh of gratitude. Now are you free of a burden so great that you could merely stagger and fall down beneath it. And it was all illusion. Nothing more. Now can the teacher of God rise up unburdened, and walk lightly on" (ACIM M-10.5:1–5).

> If you find yourself judging and blaming other people, that is mirroring back to you that there is something inside of you that you haven't dealt with, released, or forgiven yourself for. You are living in the ego's thought system and misidentifying yourself with the body and self-image.

This is how projection works. If you find yourself judging and blaming other people, that is mirroring back to you that there is something inside of you that you haven't dealt with, released, or forgiven yourself for. You are living in the ego's thought system and misidentifying yourself with the body and self-image. This is crucial to your progress, so I'm going to say it again: If you find yourself judging and blaming other people, that is mirroring back to you that there is *something* inside of you that you haven't dealt with, released, or forgiven yourself for. You are living from the ego's thought system and over-identifying yourself with the body and self-image. While in the ego, this is *not* easy to accept.

The ego will fight to keep you blaming others, judging others, finding fault with others, and even judging and punishing yourself. All in the vain effort to keep you from having to face your fear, guilt, or insecurity. Here you can use the self-study and practices to observe the ego's thought system at work, let go of the blame and judgment, and face and release the subsequent deep-seated emotions.

Let's look at the deep-seated emotions that stem from our deep-seated thoughts and beliefs all of which drive projection:

1. Fear

Initially, when we forget who and what we really are as eternal Spirit and misidentify ourselves with the mortal body and chaotic mind, we can feel enormous fear and anxiety. We believe that since we are in separate bodies, we can hurt and be hurt. We believe that since the body dies, we will die with it. We come to fear all sorts of things such as snakes, abandonment, and death. If we look more closely, we realize that our biggest fear is death of the ego, death of our false self-image because the real us, in our true nature as eternal Spirit, cannot die. This fear drives the more complex emotions of anger, guilt, jealousy, and insecurity; these emotions reflect the belief that our false self-image, or ego, can be damaged or destroyed.

2. Insecurity/Jealousy

Our identification of our "self" with the body and our self-image strengthens our belief in separation. This drives us to constantly compare ourselves to others. When we find someone we think we don't measure up to, we experience intense insecurity and sometimes jealousy. By judging and finding fault in them in an effort to preserve our false self-image, we then project our fear, guilt, and insecurity onto them.

3. Anger

We get angry or upset for their faults and possibly attack them or talk bad about them. If they put up a defense or attack back, this "proves" to us that they are wrong, bad, or unworthy—just like we thought. (And we come out looking like saints in our own ego mind, even though we set the whole thing up ourselves!)

4. Chronic Anger

We can get really angry from stuffing down these intense emotions of fear, insecurity, and guilt over a prolonged period of time as we continuously avoid them by projecting them onto others. We have no idea how to go about facing what's inside—and we fear what may happen if we do. We actually fear the death and destruction of our self-image if we admit to any of these emotions. As we refuse to look at these deeply stored emotions head-on and release them, this chronic anger can cause more discomfort and disharmony in our relationships, especially the one with ourselves.

5. Guilt

You may think that guilt is not a part of your life. "What do I have to feel guilty about?" But when you take the time to shine the light of self-study, sometimes you will find sneaky traces of guilt lurking around in your psyche. Sneaky little devils!

Whether our guilt is small or large, we carry this negative emotional energy around in our minds and bodies either consciously or unconsciously. An example of one of my own small guilts is when I throw a can straight into the garbage instead of the recycle bin. I feel guilt for being too lazy to rinse the can out so that it can be recycled. All of a sudden, thoughts are running through my head about how the landfill is going to fill up faster and this steel can might have wanted to be something else in life, but because of me, it is lying in the trash instead, unable to be recycled. This is real guilt I experience in my mind.

The events that trigger larger amounts of guilt are the more obvious ones—cheating on a spouse or partner or substance abuse. We can project our guilt onto others in an effort to make ourselves feel better or less guilty, but in reality, we are only strengthening our avoidance and making this ego mental construct seem more real.

If we were able to face and release our fear, guilt, and insecurity and not project it onto others, then we could see clearly, without the cloud of this negative emotional energy changing the way we perceive the world around us. If someone does act negatively toward us, we can see this person acting out of the ego and be able to forgive their behavior easily and effortlessly.

Let's look at different examples of projection.

Example #1

I have a friend who is brilliant. Every time I'm around her, I feel insecure because she is so intelligent, and so I project my insecurity on to her. I judge her for how bad her hair looks that day or for what she is wearing. Instead of dealing with my insecurity, I project it onto her in an effort to find fault with her. If I can let go of my insecurity, then I will be able to enjoy my friend's intelligence, rather than allow it to threaten my false self-image.

Example #2
When we carry around guilt and deep regret for wrongdoings that we have done, we are more apt to judge others for their wrongdoings in an effort to push the blame onto them. If I cheat on a partner and never deal completely with the guilt, I may judge others more harshly who cheat. If I can let go of the guilt and forgive myself, then I can forgive others who cheat and not project my guilt onto them.

Example #3
When we carry around deep fears such as abandonment, we are quicker to push people away in an effort to "save" ourselves from getting hurt again. In our efforts to prove that we are right, we project our fears onto them and then judge them for their behavior. Consequently, we see what we have projected and believe: they don't love us, and they want to leave us. Now we have proven our selves right and think that we have every right—in the ego mind's way of thinking—to push them away first. As we push this person away, it only causes more strife, reinforcing our fear of abandonment. If we can look our fear of abandonment head-on with the knowledge of our true nature being whole, perfect, and eternal, then we can let go of this deep-seated fear, stop the projection that reenforces the fear and stop pushing people away (which only strengthens our fear, loneliness, and isolation).

Negative ego thoughts and beliefs and the subsequent emotions of fear, anger, guilt, jealousy, and insecurity like to hide out in our unconscious mind. Consider this unconscious, negative emotional energy to be as destructive as an undiagnosed cancer. It can negatively affect every moment in our lives, but we have no idea what in the world is going on. All we know initially is that we feel discomfort and disharmony in some of our relationships, including the one with ourselves. Sometimes we judge and blame others. Sometimes we judge and blame ourselves, but either way, this is a clear signal that we are still living immersed in our made-up ego mental construct.

How Do We Stop Projection?

When we project negative thoughts and feelings, we are not taking responsibility for our lives by looking within and releasing the ego's thought system and the old fear, guilt, and insecurities that come with it. We are not trying to be perfect here; we are simply trying to see that the imperfections that we cannot accept in ourselves and others is the false ego-self. When we recognize our imperfections as the ego and not our true nature, this helps take away the fear, embarrassment, and shame we may feel for having these imperfections. We stop projection the same way we release *samskaras*, by utilizing the yogic self-study and practices. Here we can face our imperfections and accept and release the negative emotional energy that comes with them, rather than continue to ignore what's really happening. When we ignore and resist our false ego-self's imperfections and the negative emotional energy that comes with them, we project this negative energy onto others and suffer the subsequent discomfort and disharmony that comes from this avoidance and resistance.

Utilizing the Practice and Self-Study to Stop Projection

First, we find ourselves wanting to attack, blame, or dislike another. We come into witness consciousness, observing ourselves so that we can trace this desire to attack, blame, or dislike another back to what thoughts and beliefs are driving the emotions of fear, anger, insecurity, or guilt that may be coming up for us. If we can't do this without some pretty intense emotions coming up, then we come into a movement meditation practice and work on releasing these intense emotions through the breath and movement first.

As we release these intense emotions, we can more clearly track specific thoughts or beliefs about ourselves that are driving these emotions. We notice how silly, crazy, or downright mean these thoughts and beliefs are. As we utilize the practice to release these intense emotions, we are able to slow down and look at our negative thought patterns, beliefs, judgments, *samskaras*, and then the ego tricks and temptations that continuously pull us back in to these patterns—even when we know better.

This is not always easy. It can be extremely difficult to stop projection. According to the ego, it is so easy and so much fun to find someone else at fault and blame them for making us feel a certain way. "He did it!" Sounds like a three-year-old, doesn't it? Remember that desire for specialness? The ego in us enjoys feeling superior as it divvies out blame and judgment for all the wrongful deeds everyone else is responsible for. It actually feels good to the ego's thought system when we think we are in the right and others are in the wrong. I like being right. Unfortunately, in this made-up ego mental construct, so does everyone else!

> The ego in us enjoys feeling superior as it divvies out blame and judgment for all the wrongful deeds everyone else is responsible for.

Step 5 to Awakening: Choose Spirit Now

In witness consciousness, we can really see both sides of the fence. We observe the ego's thought system and belief system wanting to take over us, and we notice the peaceful, quiet place of Spirit. From this observant state, we can decide whether the ego or Spirit uses the mind. In other words, we have a choice! When we are tuning in to Holy Spirit via our intuition we are tuning in to the voice for God. The yogic self-study and practices only help us to tune in to this guidance to *choose Spirit now* most every time.

> From this observant state, we can decide whether the ego or Spirit uses the mind. In other words, we have a choice!

In Step 5, you are recognizing that in every moment, you have a choice which makes you responsible for the life you live. I'm going to say that again.

> In Step 5, you are recognizing that in every moment, you have a choice which makes you responsible for the life you live.

In Step 5, you are recognizing that in every moment, you have a choice which makes you responsible for the life you live.

You can choose to live immersed in the ego's thought system leading to unexpected highs and lows: feeling like a big shot, feeling like you're better or more special than others, and then feeling dissatisfied and unfulfilled, or beating yourself up by thinking you are worthless. Or you can choose to live in Spirit and experience the peace, joy and unconditional love that is your true nature and live the happy dream.

You haven't necessarily healed *all* the unconscious guilt, insecurity, and fear in your mind, but at this point, at least you can rise above it and experience awakening. Now, when the ego overwhelms you again, you have the tools and the process to fully experience it, release it, and shift back into that state of spirit and peace. Eventually, you get so good at the process that you never leave that state of peace. In reality, we can never leave this state of peace; we just feel like we do when we are immersed back in the ego mind-set.

The Choice is Always Yours

There may be a certain situation in your life in which you have a lot of anger and resentment toward someone. The ego convinces you that this

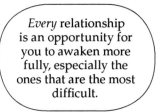

Every relationship is an opportunity for you to awaken more fully, especially the ones that are the most difficult.

particular situation doesn't count, that this particular person did do something wrong and should be blamed, judged, or punished for it. The ego will convince you that your anger and resentment toward this person really is justified. Don't let the ego pull the wool over your eyes. *Every* relationship is an opportunity for you to awaken more fully, especially the ones that are the most difficult.

On some level, we choose certain relationships to bring this stuff up so that we can release it and awaken even more fully. In every relationship, you have a choice: you can continue to blame, judge, or dislike others, or you can see this discomfort in relationships as a reminder to remember what you and this other person really are: a perfect creation of God. From there, you have a chance to work on your own fear, guilt, and insecurity. From this place, you are strong enough to quit projecting it and release it for good.

So the next time so-and-so "bothers" you, smile to yourself, and know that another step toward your awakening was just laid out in front of you. It's your choice: take a healing step forward or turn a blind eye and stay right where you are in discomfort and disharmony.

If we choose Spirit now, the light of Holy Spirit shines through and reminds us of our true nature as nothing-less-than-perfect creations of God. Now we are able to see clearly and see the miracle that we are all connected, not separate, in everyday life. Our relationships still act as mirrors, but now, we see everyone and everything as a perfect reflection of ourselves as One. Now we are living the happy dream, a life of peace and joy.

Discomfort and disharmony *or* the happy dream? Is the choice really that difficult?

I recommend *Take Me to Truth: Undoing the Ego* by Nouk Sanchez and Tomas Vieira as an excellent resource on your path to understanding projection more fully.

Insecurity and Jealousy: The Ego's Dirty Little Secrets

When I was in college, I was gossiping with friends one day when my best friend interrupted me to say, "You're just jealous!" Wow. It stopped me in my tracks. From then on, anytime I found myself ready to talk about someone, I asked myself if I could be jealous. It didn't always stop me from talking about someone, but it definitely made me more aware of my own ego, fears, and insecurities, and how they influenced me to gossip or speak condescendingly about another person in an effort to either make them look bad or me look better.

When we feel insecure and another person brings up that insecurity (maybe they are prettier, smarter, richer), we can watch as the ego bides its time searching for faults it can use to judge them to be less than we are. We are then projecting—seeing something in them that we don't like (because of *our* own insecurities) and using that to distance ourselves from this person. This strengthens the ego's belief in separation and reinforces the ego's temptation of avoidance (in this case, avoidance of the truth of what's really going on).

It is hard to look yourself in the eye and admit to feelings of fear, jealousy and insecurity, but when you do it will feel as if a huge weight has been lifted off of your shoulders. You *can* let go of that desire for specialness and inequality and the need to compete. You *can* choose Spirit now and see yourself as equal and One with others in Spirit. You *can* do this and your relationships will prosper because of it.

My Own Experience with Jealousy

I remember being extremely jealous as a kid, especially of this one friend in class. I just wanted something *bad* to happen to her so that she would disappear. I would have been so happy if I never had to see her again in my life.

I have had moments throughout my life of painful, debilitating jealousy. However, the last thing that I would ever admit to anyone was that I was jealous. That's the killer about jealousy. I would rather catch myself on fire than admit that I was jealous! So I did what every ego-minded self would do. I hated these people. I wished that they would either fall off a cliff or quit bothering me with their perfect looks (or perfect whatever) and just *go away.*

What a way to live! When there are people in your life who literally make you physically ill to be around them or you dread knowing you are going to see them, it can make your life a living hell. You know why? Because they are going to continue to come around until you quit avoiding the truth of what's really going on here.

Finally, I found ACIM. When I really started understanding this concept of projection, I was able to get to a point where I knew that this jealousy and insecurity was supposed to be showing me something inside of myself that needed healing. But I fought the idea. "No, I'm not jealous of her. She really *is* just a bitch!"

It took me years to finally be able to look myself in the mirror and admit to jealousy. It embarrassed me and I felt like I was letting myself down because I was *supposed* to be better than others. Admitting to jealousy was admitting that others might be better than me and my ego sure as hell didn't want me to do that! Hello, crazy!

As I began to take a look at all my insecurities, I realized I had an intense fear of never being good enough. I utilized my yoga practice to release this fear and release my misidentification with my ego self-image. This enabled me to admit to my jealousy and insecurity and realize that as I remembered my true nature, there was no more reason for these feelings of inadequacy. Now I was able to see people I had been previously jealous of, and feel totally at ease around them. I was no longer constantly judging them to prove to myself that I was better than them. If someone *was* acting like a bitch, now I could see their ego at play and forgive them for it rather than use that as an excuse to judge and dislike them.

> If someone *was* acting like a bitch, now I could see their ego at play and forgive them for it rather than use that as an excuse to judge and dislike them.

What I found to be even more amazing was that I loved the people I had been jealous of! I could never have admitted that before in my jealous ego mind. As I was able to forgive myself for hating them, I was then able to feel this overwhelming love and gratitude for them for being willing to be that object of hate for me in my life. On some level, they agreed to be an object of hate and jealousy for me for as long as it took, until I was finally able to experience my true nature and remember my unconditional love for them and myself.

It is really powerful when you reestablish yourself in your true nature and then can look yourself in the eye and admit to some pretty painful and embarrassing feelings. This brings comfort and harmony back to your relationships (including the one with yourself) and it sure makes life a hell of a lot easier!

An Opening to the Box I Had Been Living In

Once my divorce was final, I settled into living alone with Roxy and Cayman, my two boxers, and Scout, my cat. After a two-year hiatus, I was also able to return to my work as a massage therapist, something that I loved to do. My mentor, Denise, had asked me to join her group, and I was ecstatic!

I was having the time of my life hanging out with my coworkers who were so very refreshingly different from what I was used to. Since most of my friends at this point were married and having babies, I hung out on the weekends with my coworkers too. We had intense, deep conversations on every topic you could ever imagine. I began to see their viewpoints, which were so different from what I had grown up around. I realized that my mentor's ability to see such meaning in life was what I had been missing for so long in my own.

I had been in the mind-set of thinking that anyone who didn't fit into the box I had grown accustomed to was just "different." It always felt like an effort to try and find things in common with others to talk about if they weren't much like me. I always saw differences in others as a good reason to judge and avoid them because of my shyness and insecurity, but Denise saw past *differences* to the *beauty* in everyone. I'll never forget her going on once about how beautiful someone's nose was—and it was the biggest nose I had ever seen! She could appreciate the different features people had and try to determine what their particular ancestry might have been. She saw people with differences as interesting, a concept that my insecurity and shyness prevented me from exploring.

I was amazed! I was always judging myself and others in my mind. I always liked other people, but I never felt like I could stop the automatic judgments that arose about them. Now for the first time, my inner dialogue started to change. I started to see people differently and in a more positive light. I was able to put myself in others' shoes and know that they were absolutely no different from me. Over time, I was able to talk to people without my negative judgments clouding the way I saw them. In people I had once labeled "unattractive," I could now truly see beauty. I was able to let go of the negative judgments about myself too. No longer would a bad hair day send me on a rant in my head about how ugly and worthless I was.

During the seven years I worked with Denise and these other co-workers, my mind expanded out of its box in so many ways. I was getting used to seeing myself (and others) in a whole new light. This prepared me for what the Course would then teach me a few years later, to see past the form all together to the true nature in everyone and everything that connects us all. As I was able to shift more and more from living from ego to living from Spirit, I was finally able to put to rest the jealousy and insecurity that had plagued me for so long and find ease and harmony in relationships and in life because of it. Allelujah!

In the next chapter we will discuss yogic and course principles that come naturally as we shift more and more from ego to Spirit; principles that are a necessity for living a life awake.

CHAPTER 19

Forgiveness, Acceptance, and Calls for Love

At the time, although I saw all this clearly, I could not see how it worked; I could not see how, by accepting the self, one could go beyond the self.

—Bernadette Roberts, *The Path to No-Self: Life at the Center* (1991, 117)

Radical Acceptance=Radical Forgiveness

Accept everything, said the swami, those things we label good and those things we label bad. —Cope quotes Swami Kripalu in *The Wisdom of Yoga* (2006, 135)

Radical acceptance allows us to experience life without resistance. We are no longer building more walls with judgment and blame. Forgiveness is no longer about pardoning those who have harmed us, it's about realizing that there is nothing to forgive in the first place. If we accept that "wrongdoing" is based on the ego's thought system, we accept that there is no wrongdoing to forgive. Forgiveness and acceptance are choosing to see past the ego to the innocence in ourselves and others as One in Spirit. Unless we are saints, we *will* find ourselves acting from ego from time to time. This is where radical self-acceptance is *key*.

> Unless we are saints, we *will* find ourselves acting from ego from time to time. This is where radical self-acceptance is *key*.

170

I want to share a quote from Stephen Cope's book, *The Wisdom of Yoga*. "To whatever extent you are able to be objective in your self-observation, to that extent you will receive the light. Do not wrestle with a fault that you want to remove. Wrestling increases the disturbance of the mind and allows the excited fault to lift you up and slam you to the ground" (2006, 135). Here he is speaking of Swami Kripalu's idea of radical self-acceptance.

Cope says, "the more we push, pull, resist, the more deeply we become enmeshed in grasping, aversion, and afflicted mind. And afflicted mind can only take us deeper into suffering" (2006, 135). When we are not in an emotionally intense fight-or-flight situation with the ego, we can more easily stay in Spirit and work on studying and releasing the ego. But when the ego is triggered and we find ourselves in an emotionally intense fight-or-flight situation, sometimes we will find the ego in complete control. At this point, it is next to impossible to take the reins. Here it is best to simply stay in witness consciousness, nonjudgmentally observe our ego taking over, and forgive and accept the situation as best we can as the ego feeds off of the conflict.

> Witness-consciousness allows for us to connect with our higher self *even amidst the ego taking control*. We surrender ourselves to our higher self and allow Holy Spirit to draw us out of the ego mind gently.

This is an interesting place to be. We can see ego taking over but we remain open to the guidance of Spirit. Witness-consciousness allows for us to connect with our higher self *even amidst the ego taking control*. We surrender ourselves to our higher self and allow Holy Spirit to draw us out of the ego mind gently. If we judge or blame ourselves for our reactions, then we just find ourselves under more stress and guilt created by the ego. This is wrestling with the excited fault, that as Cope says, increases the disturbance in the mind. As we choose to accept and forgive ourselves for reacting from ego, we actually help undo more layers of this made-up ego mental construct.

> As we choose to accept and forgive ourselves for reacting from ego, we actually help undo more layers of this made-up ego mental construct.

When we are in the midst of an emotionally intense fight-or-flight situation, the ego can slam us down and make us act in ways that we are embarrassed to face. We have to trust that this situation is showing us another aspect of ego that still needs to be released within us. Initially, this is an opportunity for us to forgive ourselves for allowing ego to take over to begin with, then work on releasing our deeply embedded reactions and the emotional energy driving them through practice and self-study. At some point, we get to a point in which we can forgive ourselves and others quickly and easily. As we practice forgiveness and acceptance, we eventually find ourselves doing this automatically without getting drawn into the intense fight-or-flight situation at all.

> At some point, we get to a point in which we can forgive ourselves and others quickly and easily. As we practice forgiveness and acceptance, we eventually find ourselves doing this automatically without getting drawn into the intense fight-or-flight situation at all.

My Most Recent Struggle in a Relationship

Recently there was someone in my life who misunderstood my intentions and got very upset with me. Initially, my ego took over, and I cursed this person. Then I realized that she was genuinely upset and felt genuinely hurt. She had every right to feel that way and should have felt that way due to the things she *thought* I had done and said. I spent a lot of time trying to explain how she must have misunderstood me. She was able to understand some, but her ego wouldn't allow her to completely let it go.

This situation really angered me. My ego wanted to hear her apologize for misunderstanding me and causing this debacle in the first place. It took days, even weeks, for my ego to calm down enough for me to really be able to shine the light on what was going on here. I finally realized that I was attached to my ego self-image of being a "nice person." By her misunderstanding me and thinking I had acted in a hurtful way toward her, she was threatening this "nice person" self-image.

I realized that I needed to let go of my need for her to see me a certain way, but I *kept* feeling my ego flaring up. I wanted to attack her, fight with her and *make* her see me as a "nice person"; certainly not living up to this nice and easy self-image! I had to simply keep forgiving and accepting my thoughts and actions until eventually my ego subsided. It took awhile, but after a few weeks, I felt that I had finally shifted back into Spirit and could talk to her without the ego getting in the way.

Now my desire to explain myself to her *wasn't* coming from my ego's desire to be seen a certain way. It was coming from Spirit and *the desire to alleviate her pain* in any way that I could. With Spirit guiding, we were both able to admit to some embarrassing hurt feelings, forgive, truly let go, and move on.

Through this misunderstanding, this situation showed me that I still had this self-image I was holding on to. I realized that when my ego took control here, I couldn't let it go. *I didn't want to let it go.* I wanted to fight her rather than love her. I wanted to be *right* rather than *peaceful*.

This was such an eye-opening experience for me. I realized that I am not immune to the ego. I realized that as much as I understand the ego and as much as I have let a lot of it go, it is still able to slam me out of nowhere. This gave me an enormous amount of compassion for others and myself in dealing with this ego mind-set. This brought me to the realization that even though it's great to know how to undo the ego, it is more important to be vigilant and determined to forgive and accept ourselves and others when the ego gains control once again.

> This brought me to the realization that even though it's great to know how to undo the ego, it is more important to be vigilant and determined to forgive and accept ourselves and others when the ego gains control once again.

I trust that my higher self gave me this opportunity to be able to see how important forgiveness and acceptance really are and to explain this to people. I trust that my higher self will continue to put opportunities in my life that will help me to awaken even more. It's not always a bed of roses, but once we see clearly, we can look upon these opportunities and be grateful for what they are teaching us.

Radical Acceptance=Going beyond Self

When we accept and forgive everything, we automatically let go of all of our fears, guilt, and insecurities. We quit projecting and experience the happy dream in which we feel an inclusive sense of joy and peace.

I want to share another passage from Bernadette Roberts's book *The Path to No Self: Life at the Center*. Remember, she is the Christian contemplative who used to be a Carmelite nun. "At the time, although I saw all this clearly, I could not see how it worked; I could not see how, by accepting the self, one could go beyond the self" (Roberts 1991, 117). We need to get to a point at which we accept our "selves" so totally that we can let go of our "self" completely. We do this through radical forgiveness and radical self-acceptance.

We all want to make positive changes for our selves, but we have to be sure that we aren't simply trying to trade an undesirable self-image for a better, more positive self-image. What we need to do is totally accept our self-image *as it is now*. In doing so, we will then be able to release it and go *beyond* the self. We have to be aware that we are not simply trading our false self for a better self; we are going even beyond self, to our true nature.

This total acceptance of self allows change to come from the inside out, as opposed to a more difficult outside-in approach. The difference is that by accepting yourself totally, you let go of the ego, of the self, and all the negative emotional energy that drives the negative behavior. So you find yourself making these positive changes naturally and easily. The positive changes are no longer about building a better self-image. You are simply allowing yourself to live more of that happy dream.

Story about My Grandparents

I want to share a story now about my grandmother and her difficulty with forgiveness. We've talked about *vasanas* being those deep impressions that we carry over from one lifetime to the next. There are also *vasanas* that get passed down from generation to generation. I know that the jealousy and insecurity that my grandmother experienced in her life was passed down to my mother, to my siblings, and to me.

When I was a teenager, my grandfather was dying of lung cancer. My grandparents had been divorced a long time at this point, but apparently in their marriage, he'd had multiple affairs which, of course, only exacerbated her jealousy and insecurity. On his deathbed in his home, we were all in his room with my grandmother. We were taking turns kissing him and saying good-bye. It was then that he asked my grandmother for her forgiveness. She said no. I judged her for this. Each person in the room that day questioned how she could not forgive him as he was lying there dying of lung cancer.

It took me until my twenties to really begin experiencing my own jealousies and insecurities in a relationship. It was then that I understood how she could withhold her forgiveness. Her ego prevented her from being able to give that to him. On some level, she probably wanted to offer him that forgiveness so very badly, but she was unable to find even a crack in that ego wall that she had been building all those years to be able to extend forgiveness to him.

When I finally understood this, I was able to forgive my grandmother. By "forgive," I mean that I was able to see past her ego façade and see the innocence in her. Once I did this, I was then able to let go of a huge chunk of my own ego in terms of insecurity and jealousy. In going through this, I felt a deep connection with my grandmother and a deep sense of peace. I was able to forgive and see past the ego to her innocence and my own.

Global Forgiveness Lessons

Forgiveness becomes more difficult for us when we think of terrorist acts that affect a lot of people and generate a lot of fear all at once, such as the attack on the World Trade Center towers. It's so easy to feel separate from people who come from across the globe, who look different, talk different, and who have different beliefs. At some point, we have to see past the crimes that these people committed and see the innocence even in them. This doesn't mean that they shouldn't serve time for their crimes; it means that the hate, anger, and blame that drove them to commit such an act to begin with, is not then perpetuated in us with our own hate, anger, and blame. If we can forgive them and see the peace and love in them, we then stop that hate in its tracks. We then stop the ego's ability to further our separation, and with that, we take away our fear of something like this happening again.

The truth is most of us don't know what to expect. But if we go around living in a state of fear and stress all the time, waiting for something bad to happen to us, we lose the fullness of life. When you can forgive these people and extend peace and love toward them, the fear is then lost in the process. Now you know that whatever happens, however terrible, can be forgiven. Now you know that whatever happens, peace and love can shine through. This helps to take the fear out of it.

This is not necessarily easy to do, because the ego will bring up an enormous amount of resistance. The ego will pull out every stop to make you believe you are definitely separate and different from people who commit terrorist acts. It will convince you that anger, judgment, and sometimes even hate towards them is justified in these situations. As long as you allow the ego to pull the wool over your eyes, you will live with the discomforts of fear, anger, hate, and blame—and wonder why you feel stressed, anxious, and fearful.

> The ego will pull out every stop to make you believe you are definitely separate and different from people who commit terrorist acts. It will convince you that anger, judgment, and sometimes even hate towards them is justified in these situations. As long as you allow the ego to pull the wool over your eyes, you will live with the discomforts of fear, anger, hate, and blame—and wonder why you feel stressed, anxious, and fearful.

Answering a Call for Love with Love

When a person "attacks" us, ACIM calls it a "call for love." When we attack back or defend ourselves, we put up another ego wall strengthening the ego's belief in separation and fortifying the entire made-up mental construct. When we decide to answer with love, we forgive this person by seeing through the ego to the innocence in them. We watch as the ego walls and mental construct come tumbling down. When we answer with love, we are remembering who we are as one in eternal Spirit with no walls, no lines, and no separation.

Not too long ago, my husband and I were watching an Oprah rerun where she was giving away cars to every member of the audience. Everybody was getting emotional and tearing up as they were taken outside to see their new cars.

I asked my husband, "Could you imagine being able to do that for people?" He replied, "It would be awesome." In that moment, I realized that everyone has in their hearts the desire to be able to give like that, and yet there is so much strife in the world. If you ask anyone what they would do if they won a million dollars, they usually say they want to pay off their debt. But most people then want to give something to someone. They want to give to someone in need.

Then I realized that we all *do* have the ability to give others a gift even more beautiful than a new car. We have the ability to give others the gift of seeing past their ego to their true nature within! We have the ability to give the gift of seeing their innocence, no matter what the ego has driven them to do, *and* we can do the same for ourselves. We have the ability to answer these calls *for* love *with* love. And that's a real gift to give someone!

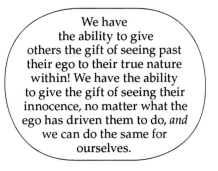

We have the ability to give others the gift of seeing past their ego to their true nature within! We have the ability to give the gift of seeing their innocence, no matter what the ego has driven them to do, *and* we can do the same for ourselves.

Experience God

Tom and Linda Carpenter have a great CD collection called *Healing the Dream*. I want to share a passage that Tom shares in this CD collection. You have to imagine that this passage that I'm about to share is God speaking to Tom Carpenter, because Tom explains that he heard God speaking to him through his mind.

"I speak to you with the voice of every brother, but it is not in his words that you will hear what I speak, for it is there that you have denied me. But as he calls for love and your willingness to answer are you made one. And it is there that you will always find me." (Carpenter, Linda and Tom 2007). You can learn more about Tom Carpenter's experience at *www.TheForgivenessMovement.org.*

When you decide to forgive someone rather than throw up that wall of separation, hate, judgment, and blame, then you experience what yoga calls union, Oneness, bliss. This is where you find God.

What Does This Mean?

When we drop our walls of separation and choose love over judgment, love over blame, love over a good fight, love over fear, or love over the ego's attempts to isolate us (which in the long run only make us more lonely, sad, and depressed), we experience the connection and the divinity within every aspect of creation. The best part about it is this: It is *never* too late to see differently. It is *never* too late to choose Spirit. It is *never* too late to see the miracle. It is *never* too late to experience God.

Every time you choose to judge another, you are really judging yourself.

Every time you choose to judge another, you are strengthening the belief that we are separate and isolated from each other.

I want to share my favorite quote from ACIM:

> When you meet anyone, remember it is a holy encounter. As you see him you will see yourself. As you treat him you will treat yourself. As you think of him you will think of yourself. Never forget this, for in him you will find yourself or lose yourself. Whenever two Sons of God meet, they are given another chance at salvation. Do not leave anyone without

giving salvation to him and receiving it yourself. For I am always there with you, in remembrance of you. (ACIM T-8. III.4:1–8)

What a beautiful quote. That's what this is all about. In any given moment, whomever is in front of us is giving us the opportunity to have a holy encounter by dropping our ego walls and *seeing* them clearly.

Now you can see every opportunity for forgiveness as a potential gift of experiencing God. Be grateful to the person who presents you with that opportunity. It's okay when you blow it and you can't seem to drop those walls. Simply forgive yourself and accept your ego's actions; in time, the Holy Spirit will help you to choose differently. It's never too late!

> Now you can see every opportunity for forgiveness as a potential gift of experiencing God. Be grateful to the person who presents you with that opportunity.

Never Too Late

My mom had a falling out with two of her siblings when my grandmother died. These three maintained a chilly silence for almost a decade—until today. As I'm writing this, we just found out yesterday that my mom has lung cancer. My brother contacted Mom's sister (our aunt) to let her know. She immediately asked if Mom would be okay if she came by the hospital. Mom agreed, so her sister visited. They are both longtime smokers (although my aunt quit a few years ago to smoke the electronic cigarette). When my aunt walked into the room, Mom said, "I always thought *you* would be the one to get lung cancer." The ice was broken. Not long after, they were both sitting on Mom's hospital bed toking on some e-cigarettes my aunt had brought. After ten years, they were able to drop the walls of the past and simply be with each other. When we are finally faced with the realization that this life is short and that this experience is not forever, we can much more easily drop down to the bare bones of what really matters. And that is this union, this connection with each other and love for each other that is unbreakable.

179

Ginger Graf Dunaway

My Story with Forgiveness

I want to share a story with you of my own recent forgiveness opportunity. I had just finished up my second workshop for Choose Spirit Now here in Mobile. I had just finished telling everybody to be aware, that the ego likes to rear its ugly head once you start to study it and watch it. What happened? The next day, my ego reared its ugly head.

Someone I love dearly gave me a huge forgiveness opportunity. They told me about something that they did, and all of a sudden, I had this huge rush of emotion well up. I was right back in those same emotions I had felt so often with my ex-husband. I was fearful, I was insecure, and I wanted to shut down and run the other way. I shifted into that witness-consciousness state, and I was able to become pretty peaceful. I began simply watching all of this happen. I was watching the ego rear its ugly head. I was watching myself wanting to shift into this drama that had been so much a part of my life for so long in my twenties.

Today, as I remember this encounter, I realize that the ego was trying to drum up all of these emotions of self-pity, insecurity, and blame—and the deep desire to hold a grudge. It was like watching someone trying to spark some kindling into a fire, but it simply wasn't catching fire for me. I was watching it happen, and I was listening to the ego trying to manipulate me into going into that state of shutdown and putting that wall up. "Oh, poor Ginger, it's happening to you again. See? You can't trust anyone. Poor you. You're that little innocent child again that bad things happen to. No one is here to save you. No one is here to help you. What is life all about anyway? What is the meaning of any of this? You might as well put an end to it. No one really loves you."

But this time, it wasn't working! The light inside shone through it. Believe me, it wasn't easy. It took me a whole day of moving in and out of this witness-consciousness state and wondering what decision I was going to make. Was I going to allow myself to be sucked into the ego drama and become depressed and hold a grudge? Or was I going to make a different choice? I finally was able to say, "You know what, I'm not going there. I'm going to choose to forgive here. I'm going to choose to not go into my habitual feelings of disappointment, depression, unworthiness, and meaninglessness."

The most amazing thing happened. I realized that as much as I did want to hold that grudge for a week and get sucked into that negative pattern, it was so much easier when I decided to forgive and release it. It was like watching the ego shrivel up and disappear (just like the Wicked Witch's feet shriveled up under the house in *The Wizard of Oz*)! The ego lost its power and was gone, poof. I was then able to go to this person and tell them how grateful I was for them to give me this opportunity. I also realized that what this person did was not such a big deal at all when I was able to see it without my samskaras and vasanas getting in the way and blowing it out of proportion.

In that moment, I realized that not only did I forgive this person, but I also was able to forgive myself. I realized that I had let go of a huge chunk of insecurity and fear that I had been holding on to for so long, one that I had been working on releasing for so long. I was also able to forgive my ex-husband, the one I had blamed for the fear, insecurity, and pattern of drama that really began for me in childhood. This was an amazing moment for me. I was so grateful for it because I would have never known that I still had all of this stored emotion and pattern to release without this forgiveness opportunity to bring it forward.

I share this with you to tell you that this stuff works. In real life and in real situations, *this stuff works.* I was able to forgive—maybe not immediately, but eventually, and I was even able to be grateful for it. As we strengthen our relationship and trust in Holy Spirit, our higher self, we are more apt to be able to hear it over the cries, whines, and pleas of the ego while in these highly charged emotionally intense moments so that we can then *choose Spirit now.*

Relationships as a Gauge for the Ego

Forgiveness opportunities in a relationship are the best gauge to see how far you've come in your awakening. There is no need to judge yourself if you are unable to forgive immediately. Simply know that you can make a different choice—to forgive—next time. Although it seems difficult in the beginning, in actuality, forgiveness is the easiest and most loving choice for yourself and for anyone else involved. And just as my mom took years to finally forgive my dad, sometimes it takes that amount of time to realize fully that the pain and the suffering in our lives is not always from what others have "done" to us, but rather from our deepest fears that eventually must be released. As we remember our true nature, we easily face and release these fears. Forgiveness becomes second nature, and *all* of our relationships take a turn for the better.

CHAPTER 20

Relationships as the Key to Awakening

> Going to live on a mountaintop for the rest of your life would
> be easy. The difficult thing to do is to stay here in the middle
> of life and various relationships and really put yourself out
> there.
>
> —My mother, Carole Graf

Relationships Give Us Opportunities to Awaken

When someone seemingly slaps us in the face, our instinctual ego
reaction is to slap back. When we find someone we don't measure
up against, our instinctual ego reaction is to judge them and find
fault with them. When we are making decisions based on someone
else's expectations of us, our instinctual reaction is to blame them for
influencing us to live a life that we really don't want to live. When you
feel that gut-wrenching, potent, and powerful urge to fight back with
all you've got, judge a person out of jealousy, or blame someone for your
guilt, you should *open your eyes* to this opportunity to awaken.

Relationships are the key to awakening. They reveal the deepest
guilt, fear, and insecurities that we may not have otherwise known
were there. This is what keeps us from awakening totally and living
the happy dream. Now you can see every forgiveness opportunity
presented to you as a time to be grateful for that relationship as it
presents another key to your awakening. Once you experience union,
bliss, and the happy dream, there are no more walls and, hence, no
need for keys. Now you can stay put in the middle of life and various
relationships and experience no discomfort or disharmony because you

are living awake. *Now* you *can* go live on a mountain top and meditate for the rest of your life in complete harmony and bliss if you really want to. Now there is nothing hiding out that needs to be mirrored back to you for you to let go of!

Easy Way Out

After my divorce, when I was single, I felt like I would never find someone wonderful to share my life with again. I'll never forget being at our beach house and telling my mom and my sister, Suzette, that if I didn't find anyone in the next five years, I was going to live on a mountain and meditate for the rest of my life.

My Mom said the most brilliant thing to me which helped me to realize that I was attempting to take the easy road out through that old ego temptation of avoidance. She said, "Ginger, going to live on a mountaintop for the rest of your life would be easy. The difficult thing to do is to stay here in the middle of life and various relationships and really put yourself out there." I'm not saying people who meditate on mountaintops are taking the easy road, but *I* just wasn't ready for that. I still *needed* relationships to further me on my path. The truth is that until we learn to shift out from the ego entirely, we need relationships, especially the most difficult ones, to reveal more of our unconscious ego.

Special vs. Holy Relationships

Special relationships are based on conditional love. One person expects the other person to behave a certain way, to fulfill a need. When that person doesn't live up to the expected behavior, the other one gets upset, sometimes to the point of ending the relationship. They are seeing each other out of ego rather than Spirit. Most of us are living in special relationships.

Holy relationships are based on unconditional love. Each person remembers his or her true nature and is totally free to be who he or she is in this life. Each person is totally accepted. Each person sees innocence in the other, no matter what, and if they don't, they quickly realize the ego's work and forgive and accept. They go to Holy Spirit together or individually for guidance throughout their relationship.

Special relationships can be turned into holy relationships with the help of Holy Spirit. You can have a holy relationship with just one person going to Holy Spirit, going to their higher self for guidance. And this isn't just about a marital relationship or a boyfriend/girlfriend relationship. This is about parents, children, siblings, and friends; any relationship can become a holy relationship.

In my own relationship with my husband, Mark, we both study the ego, making it much easier to communicate with this knowledge. We are both able to see the ego at work in ourselves and each other and to look past it (most of the time) to the innocence in each other. If he snaps at me, I can see it is his ego. I can see past that to the innocence in him. If I snap at him, he can see that it is my ego and see past that to the innocence in me. Sometimes we get stuck in ego and blame the other for something, but it's never long before one of us gets clear and reminds the other that the ego has put one over on us again.

Meeting Mark

My husband does have an ego. But the first thing I ever noticed and loved about him was that he doesn't have much of one. His stepmother, Jo, has been one of my massage clients for years, and she had been mentioning that Mark and I needed to meet for about two years. He was into Tai Chi, and since I was into yoga, she thought we would have something in common. I still remember swiveling around in the desk chair where I worked as I got up the nerve to call Jo and ask if Mark was still single.

After that phone call, Jo gave my cell number to Mark. Now my first clue as to how little ego he had was the fact that he called me the very next day. I expected to have to wait at least a week. I had been reading *The Disappearance of the Universe* at this point and knew how important it was for me to work on overcoming the ego in myself, not to mention the importance of finding someone who would be similarly inclined.

We had a date that weekend. I wish I could say the rest is history, but it wasn't. Mark did everything right. He was cute, he was nice, and he called all the time. He made it known he liked me and he even told me two weeks in, "Girl, I'm going to marry you someday!"

But because I had been divorced, I was scared of making a mistake again. I allowed fear and the ego to take over to the point that I couldn't make heads or tails of my feelings for Mark. He was everything I had been wanting in a guy, but for some reason, I was scared to move forward. Worse, a guy I had dated before was calling again and wanting to see me.

What *The Disappearance of the Universe* helped me to do at that point was to really see the ego (or lack thereof) working in these two guys. The other guy had seen Mark and me out together, and suddenly, he wanted me back. I had a conversation with Mark about talking to the other guy and hearing him out. He told me to take my time to figure things out, and that he would be waiting. What guy says that? I now know that he was going crazy inside, but he trusted himself enough to be able to let go and give me the space and freedom I needed.

That in itself told me what I needed to know about Mark Dunaway. I never could put my finger on it until then, but this was what I wanted in a guy. He was sure of himself, but not in an egotistical way. I sensed he had trust in something higher in life, no doubt from his studies of the Tao.

So Mark and I started dating. Three months later, he moved in. A month after that, we were engaged. Four months after that, we were happily married on a beach in Costa Rica. After beginning our study of ACIM together several years later, we both realized that we had found in each other a desire to let go of our special relationship so that we could move into a holy relationship. This allowed us both to make mistakes, but we kept our focus on the common goal to see through the illusion and live our lives awake.

All the Little Things

Every now and then, Mark goes downstairs and makes himself a sandwich before work. He drops a lot of crumbs on the counter and doesn't clean them up. I find myself going into the ego's thought system, where all of a sudden I'm judging him and blaming him, tallying up all the other things he's done around the house that bother me. I have to stop myself, recognize that the ego is taking control over my mind, and ask for guidance from Holy Spirit to shift out of this and forgive. My husband is a wonderful, amazing man. For me to find blame and judge him for leaving a few crumbs on the counter (okay, socks too) is just a testament to how manipulative and crazy the ego can be.

This happens a lot in relationships. It's not always the big things that destroy a relationship. Sometimes it's all the little things that keep adding up. If you can understand how the ego mind works, you can catch all these little things building up and begin to work on releasing them. You ask Holy Spirit for guidance in allowing you to see past the ego to the innocence in that person. (And then you hire a really great housekeeping service!)

To Stay or Not to Stay

We are not always *meant* to stay in relationships. We are not being asked to tough it out no matter what. Relationships should not be tough. They help mirror back to us what we need to let go of with our own ego, *but sometimes*, what we *need* is to *detach* and *let go* when a relationship is not serving our higher purpose of learning to identify with our higher self. We have to strengthen our relationship and trust in our higher self, so that we know when we are being guided to stay and when we are being guided to leave. Don't get caught up in the ego manipulating you by saying to you, "If you were a really forgiving, loving person, you would stay in this relationship." This is not the case! You can still forgive and accept and see the innocence in someone, but you have to be open to your guidance. If it's telling you to move out of that relationship, then do so without a hefty dose of guilt attached.

Even though it may look disastrous for the other person, if we are being guided to leave, then ultimately this is the best choice for the other person too. You can still love them, forgive them, and support them without being in a relationship with them—and sometimes, this will be the best thing you can do for both of you.

Sometimes staying in the relationship is an awakening opportunity for us. But if we cannot let go of our judgment of the other person, find ourselves overcome with jealousy or insecurity, and/or find ourselves in an ongoing negative environment, then stepping out may be the better option.

If you are unsure what to do, practice a guided relaxation with a clear intention to be guided as to whether you should stay or leave. When you are done, see if the answer doesn't come to you as clear as a bell. When we go into that altered state, we should come back with clear guidance. If you are not getting a clear answer, then maybe you are not ready to make a final decision. Just know that you can love, forgive, and extend peace to anyone without having to be in a partner relationship with them.

If we were all saints, then we could stay in any relationship without it affecting us, but until we have undone our ego completely, it is not always the best option. Relationships are the key to awakening, but every so often we need to step out of a relationship to keep moving forward on our path. Allow Holy Spirit, your own higher self, to give you the strength to follow through with whatever decision is best for you.

In the next chapter, we will learn what truth-speaking is all about and how chant helps open us up for more of it.

CHAPTER 21

Truth-Speaking and Chant

When you speak the truth, it feeds and brightens your Spirit.
When you don't, it dims your Spirit.
—Ana Forrest *Fierce Medicine* (2011, 76)

Stand in Truth

In her book, *Fierce Medicine,* Ana Forrest says the following:

> Truth Speaking—speaking from a place of deep honesty and
> compassion—propels us into a very rich field of feeling. Every
> time we speak truth, it shudders through the cobwebs and
> dimness in our lives, tapping us back in to the Beauty in our
> world, in ourselves, and in each other. How incredibly sweet it
> is to be able to talk about what's really important, stepping out
> from behind our façades and the little stupid conversations
> we're taught are a necessary social lubricant. When we speak
> truth to each other, once we get past the shock, it kindles the
> desire to hear the truth coming back at us. (2011, 76)

Ana Forrest also says, "When you speak the truth, it feeds and brightens
your Spirit. When you don't, it dims your Spirit. Don't you want to live
in a way that brightens your Spirit? To take a deep breath and feel
what's rocketing and roiling around in your core? What a delight!"
(2011, 76)

Truth-speaking is all about dropping those ego walls and façades
and being real with each other, having real conversations. For the last
several years, I have been asked to speak at my old high school about

yoga and meditation. I'll never forget how nervous I was that first year, as I prepared to talk to the teenagers and remembered how judgmental they can be due to their own insecurities.

As I began my talk, some of the kids were shifting around and even giggling as I discussed the history of yoga. But they began listening up as soon as I started talking about my own thoughts and fears that I had had at their age. I told them how, as a teenager, there was a voice in my head that always seemed to be judging me or other people. This voice, my ego, was constantly working to tear me down or build me up in my mind. I gave them some examples. *Her hair looks disgusting. Who does he think he is? I'll never be as pretty as her. I'll never be as smart as him. I'm so much thinner than she is.*

The kids quit shifting around. They were intently looking at me as if I had read their minds. I went on to explain to them that these judgmental thoughts were their ego and not their true nature, which is wholly nonjudgmental and all-loving. It was as if I could see a part of them, the part that not only wanted to hear this but *needed* to hear this perk up.

I told them about my own depression in high school and how I felt so sad and alone and could never explain why. I explained my inability to be content and happy in the present moment. I told them that I was always wishing for the weekend to get here or waiting to look in the mirror and see someone pretty staring back at me. By this time, I can tell you they were rapt. I knew at that moment, every single one of them had felt the same way at some point. And I knew that what had finally helped me to "get it" could help them too.

Children are very present and in the moment. They are in awe of everything that they see. But as they develop into teenagers, they shift into that total ego state of now having responsibilities in this world, having expectations placed upon them by parents and teachers, and dealing with peer pressure. It's very important for us to understand how the ego works in our own lives, so we can then help our children to understand how the ego works in theirs. We need to have these real conversations with our kids and lay the groundwork for them to be able to live their lives awake.

Give the gift of truth-speaking, not just to your kids but to yourself and others. We need to ask Holy Spirit to guide us to say the right thing to open that door, drop those walls, and have real, meaningful conversations with people. I guarantee most people are eager for that door to be open for them too.

> We need to ask Holy Spirit to guide us to say the right thing to open that door, drop those walls, and have real, meaningful conversations with people.

Remember, it's not about getting drawn into gossip or sucked into other people's negative emotional energy. It's about listening to them fully. Then, rather than getting drawn into their story, give them another alternative in perception. Speak the truth with them about the ego. If it's someone you know will have a lot of resistance to these concepts, then simply hold the truth in your mind for them, something we will talk about in the next chapter.

Most importantly, keep in mind that this is about being open and supportive for people and giving them an alternate perception, not about "being right" or changing their minds. My dad is always great at truth-speaking with his kids. I am grateful that he has not simply nodded throughout my life as I went on and on about all my woes in the world. He always spoke up about how the ego might be playing out in my life. At first, it was difficult to hear. Over time, I realized that the discomfort I felt hearing his words was the discomfort of the ego wanting to be special again and again.

If my dad had not been so honest with me over the years, I would not be as far as I am now in understanding the ego. For that, I am truly grateful. But again, he is my dad and probably the easiest person in my life, besides my mom, for me to be able to hear the truth from.

Chant

Chant is devotional singing that has been done for thousands of years across many different religions and spiritual traditions. A particular Indian chant concert called a *kirtan* is a big part of *bhakti* yoga, or the yoga of devotion. In a *kirtan*, mantras are chanted in Sanskrit, a vibrational language. Chanting a mantra (a meaningful phrase) over and over is said to have an effect on us through the vibration. We actually begin to experience the meaning of the mantra we are chanting. Some mantras can be considered love songs to God. They remind us of our connection with God and to each other. There are many different ones, and you may find that you are drawn to different mantras and their meanings at different times in your life.

In yoga, chant is a form of *pranayam* (breath-work) practice. Awareness on the breathing allows a mantra to be chanted easily from a seated posture. Chanting as a breath-work practice helps to open up the fifth chakra, the throat chakra, clearing it of stagnant, negative emotional energy that gets stuck there from holding back in different ways: in what we want to say to people, in experiencing our emotions, and then in expressing ourselves emotionally. Chanting clears this stagnant energy, releases a lot of anger and frustration, and allows us to begin expressing ourselves emotionally in a clear and calm manner. Once you have cleared out any negative emotional energy through chanting, you more easily pick up on the meanings of these love songs to God. You are then filled with a sense of connection, harmony, and love that is enormously uplifting.

If anybody is skeptical about how chant might affect us vibrationally, take a look at quantum physics. Several years ago, scientists came up with string theory in which they hypothesized that the smallest particle that we are made of is a tiny vibrating filament. With this possibility, you can imagine how the vibration of chant or words and music in general can greatly affect our being.

We can explain our ability to experience the vibration and meaning of chants further by looking at experiments done by Dr. Masaru Emoto. When Dr. Emoto observed frozen water under a microscope, he found different patterns of crystals. He then observed these water crystals while performing different experiments over them such as praying, speaking particular words, and playing different types of music. He discovered that if positive words—such as *love* and *gratitude*—are spoken over the crystals, they take on a beautiful snowflake-like design, and if negative words—such as "you disgust me"—are spoken, the crystals take on a random, chaotic design. At the time this book was published, full details and illustrations from this intriguing experiment could be found at *www.masaru-emoto.net/english/water-crystal.html*. (Emoto 2010)

These experiments were done over frozen water, but when you think about the human body being comprised of 50 to 65 percent water, it seems probable that the meaning of positive and negative words affects us not just on a psychological and emotional level, but on a basic physical level as well. Most people can feel a difference in the energy in the body when confronted with words of anger and stress versus words of love and peace. When you think about how words could have such a powerful effect on our being, you realize that chanting these love songs to God in an ancient, vibrational language such as Sanskrit might truly have a positive effect on us on many different levels.

When you attend a call-and-response chant, or *kirtan* (Indian chant) concert, you can't help but notice how wonderful you feel afterward. At a *kirtan,* you are not there just to listen to and watch the musicians, you are there to participate with them also. As the vocalist sings the chant, the audience then repeats it. There is a very different experience between simply listening to the chant and actually participating by chanting the response with the audience. By participating with the musicians you are experiencing the meaning of the chant in a very intimate way. Chanting can lift us out of the ego's thought system easily as we experience the meaning of these sacred chants in kirtan.

Any music lover can tell you that music can take you into very different feelings of joy, sadness, or anger, depending on the lyrics and the way the instruments are played. I have experimented with it myself. When I listen to only chant CDs in my car, my whole life is affected positively. As soon as I whip out an old song that reminds me of my days of depression and drama, I sense these emotions creeping back into my day-to-day life. I know that things can only affect us negatively while in the ego's thought system, but since I am not out of it completely, I realize that I can get dragged back in quite easily by something as simple as listening to certain songs from my past. Be aware of this in your own life and take the time to weed out anything that only takes you back down into the ego's blues, anger, or depression.

In every yoga class at Kripalu, we chanted "om" three times after coming out of *Savasana,* relaxation pose. In one particular class, I went so deep into relaxation that I did not realize the teacher had asked everyone to sit back up in preparation for the chant. I came around just as the other sixty people began the lovely "A-U-M" sound. Each of the three times they chanted "om," I felt a part of my being (not my physical body) literally rise about two to three feet off the ground and vibrate

> Chanting is simply another yoga practice that enables us to let go and go beyond the ego, remembering that we are more than this body and this mind. We are Spirit: whole, perfect, and eternal.

with the chant. It was such an amazing experience and truly a gift in showing me that I was much more than just this physical body. Chanting is simply another yoga practice that enables us to let go and go beyond the ego, remembering that we are more than this body and this mind. We are Spirit: whole, perfect, and eternal.

Story: My Experience with Chanting

My first experience with chanting was at Kripalu, where I went for my yoga-teacher training back in 2006. My two wonderful teachers, Devarshi and Megha, led the chant for the more than sixty people in my class. When we chanted, we all sat in a semicircle and chose one of several small instruments to play. Megha brought out her harmonium and set it on the floor in front of her. She started to play, and everyone began to chant. My classmates began closing their eyes and chanting and swaying to the rhythm.

I realized in that moment that I was stuck! All I could think was that I had found myself in some *Saturday Night Live* skit in which I had been transported back in time to the '70s. I sat there thinking, *Holy moley, what have I gotten myself into?*

Chanting was a huge challenge for me. I had trouble sitting in this circle with sixty people and letting go enough to sing Sanskrit words. I had trouble allowing the rhythm to overtake me so that I could begin swaying with the rest of them. I was so stuck in all this judgment and insecurity that I couldn't even move, let alone chant.

In the past, I had alcohol or drugs to help me find that dance in my step, but now I was stone-cold sober. I was scared to be judged on how I looked when I sang. I was scared of moving awkwardly as I tried to sway to the music. I was one big ball of fear!

But as I looked around at these wonderful people I was getting to know—people from late teens to early seventies, with dreads to tattoos, from beautiful to not-so-beautiful—I noticed that some of them probably felt the exact same way I did. They probably had the same fears and insecurities that I did. But *they were trying.*

Some of them were chanting freely and allowing the rhythm of the chant to overtake them, so their movement actually began to draw me in. I was getting in tune with the synergy of the group. Little by little, my fears began to subside. My ego began to soften. My walls began to drop lower. My chanting got louder. I began to hear my own voice. And the most amazing thing happened: all of this energy that I had been using to hold back from expressing myself throughout my life began to free up.

The childhood drama that was so emotionally straining and draining as a child was never to be spoken about. We were told to keep it a secret. I don't know exactly when it started as a child, but I remember the tremendous weight of holding back when it came to expressing myself. I can still recall the "breath-holding" feeling of being too damned scared to express myself in any way. For years, I felt as if I had a huge clamp over my throat. *Not anymore!*

Chanting was such an unexpected life-changing practice for me, and it continued to work its magic over the next several years. The chant I was most drawn to was the "so hum" ("I am that I am") chant. I chanted it every chance I could: walking the labyrinth at Kripalu, driving down the road, or just silently in my mind.

Are you someone who thinks, "Humph, chant? Not going to do it. Not for me"? If so, take a moment to notice if there is ego resistance coming up in you. Can you shine the light on those fears and insecurities holding you back from experiencing something so amazing as this process of chanting? *Don't allow the ego to keep you from the gift that chanting can give to you.* Don't allow the ego to trick you into supporting its own self-preservation. If you want another opportunity to release more ego and experience God, this is it. And even though the experience of a real live kirtan is amazing, you *can* chant with a CD in the privacy of your own home and still benefit greatly.

In the next chapter we will discuss how we stay with this process of moving out of the made-up ego mental construct when it sometimes feels like the people around us and the world around us keep trying to pull us back in.

PART III

Beyond the Ego Cloud

CHAPTER 22

Be a Truth-Holder

Be willing to be that light. Sit in chaos and turmoil and say there is an alternative.

—Tom Carpenter, *Healing the Dream* CD (Carpenter and Carpenter 2007)

Discerning the Ego Working in Others

"If you perceive his errors and accept them, you are accepting yours. If you want to give yours over to the Holy Spirit, you must do this with his." (ACIM T-9.III.5:2–3)

"Your brother is as right as you are, and if you think he is wrong you are condemning yourself." (ACIM T-9.III.5:6)

When you are initially trying to discern the ego working in yourself, you will notice how easy it is to see it working in other people. If you find yourself judging them for it, it's just a sure sign of the ego working in you also, to turn this process against you. Don't let the ego trick you into seeing your brother as "less" when ego shows up in him. Practice stopping the judgment in its tracks; simply resolve to be okay with the discernment. If you have trouble with this, ask for Holy Spirit's guidance to show you the light that is connecting you both.

Gary Renard quotes Pursah in his book, *The Disappearance of the Universe:* "We said in our first visit that you save the world by concentrating on your own forgiveness lessons, not somebody else's" (Renard 2004, 245).

Again and again, your ego will want to suck you into this manipulation. It's a relief to turn the light of self-study *off* of yourself and onto someone else. *That is not your job.* Your job is to focus *on your own* forgiveness lessons. When you see the ego rise up in other people, *that is your forgiveness lesson.* See past that to the innocence in them and hold that truth in your mind for them. Once you know your ego is not pulling the strings, then truth-speaking may be an option. When in doubt, always ask for guidance from Holy Spirit.

> When you see the ego rise up in other people, *that is your forgiveness lesson.* See past that to the innocence in them and hold that truth in your mind for them.

Be a Truth-Holder for Your Brother

When someone you know is going through a trial or hardship in life and you know they are down and out, imagine enveloping them with a sense of peace and love, the essence of our true nature. You don't have to say a word (and most of the time, you shouldn't). It is difficult for people to see clearly when they are suffering in the ego's thought system. When we truly believe that we are perfect and one in Spirit, then we can look on others with no hidden pity or hidden judgments for what they may be going through. In that, you free them.

> When we truly believe that we are perfect and one in Spirit, then we can look on others with no hidden pity or hidden judgments for what they may be going through. In that, you free them.

When we know the truth of our whole, perfect, and eternal nature and can hold that truth in our minds for others, it helps to free their minds from the ego's thought system. Others *will* pick up on the fact that you are not buying into the ego's thought system by pitying them or feeling sorry for them. Their ego may pout when they realize that you are not reinforcing their drama. *But* on some level, they are picking up on the strength in you and the strength you see in them by

> *But* on some level, they are picking up on the strength in you and the strength you see in them by remembering their true nature for them. And that's a real gift to give to someone.

remembering their true nature for them. And that's a real gift to give to someone.

Compassion is not about being sad or pitying people. It's about empowering them by sending them love and reminding them, usually through silence, that we are all more than a body and more than this world. We are Spirit: whole, perfect, and eternal.

When I first started studying these concepts, I felt like they were a little harsh. It was difficult to find a balance between wanting to justify and validate people's feelings but not tie them to the ego at the same time. There was a period of time when I actually felt emotionless when people told me their stories. I couldn't feel any empathy because I could see their ego plain as day at work in them. To be honest, it felt good to *not* get sucked into their story. But what I finally realized is that the ego was tricking me again.

I had been judging people for allowing their egos to rule. As a result, I was "punishing" them by withholding validation. I had been sucked back into my ego through judgment and hypocrisy. That is how manipulative and conniving the ego can be. That's when I realized that I could not do this alone. Just as ACIM tells us again and again, *I needed Holy Spirit's help.* Holy Spirit brought me to the realization that I could be compassionate without getting sucked into the pity and the drama that only strengthens the ego's thought system.

> Holy Spirit brought me to the realization that I could be compassionate without getting sucked into the pity and the drama that only strengthens the ego's thought system.

I want to share another quote from Tom Carpenter's *Healing the Dream* DVD that will really help put this in perspective:

> There is no heart, there is no love in your continuing to look at something of pain in the world and feel sadness. That is not the purpose of your compassion. You may look at someone's pain and have the desire to end that pain. That is a desire to be compassionate, but then you must recognize what it is that can bring an end to that pain. And it will not be in your crying or in your sorrow over what you seem to be witnessing, but it will be in your willingness to hold a different awareness that the one who seems to be suffering

pain has an alternative. And you, you can be the one who is the presence of that alternative. You can hold an awareness that they need not suffer. And the way that you hold that awareness is to see in them the light that they were created to be and not the darkness that they have made for themselves. And because we sit here sharing the same mind, not with minds that are connected, but sharing the same mind, your awareness and your desire to reach out to them, which is the disowned part of you, makes that possibility of being at peace and being free of suffering a very real opportunity. (Carpenter and Carpenter 2007)

Wow. This is a passage we should be re-reading every day.

Truth-Speaking vs. Being a Truth-Holder

There will be people who are open to truth-speaking and open to having conversations with you about the ego. But there will also be people who are not. Always ask for guidance from Holy Spirit as to when is the best time to have a conversation with someone and when it is best to simply hold the truth in your mind for them. Either way, make sure you are coming from Spirit rather than ego, so that peace will prevail. If you begin a conversation and ego gets involved, pause, let it go, and go back to simply holding the truth in your mind.

> If you begin a conversation and ego gets involved, pause, let it go, and go back to simply holding the truth in your mind.

Be a Truth-Holder for the World

When something traumatic happens to you or in the world in general, remember not to allow the ego to draw you into fear, pity, anger, or sorrow. Remember to see *everyone* as equal and one in Spirit, even the people who are responsible. Allow compassion to fill your heart and your mind, as you send peace to *everyone* involved and remind yourself that they are Spirit: whole, perfect, and eternal. This state of peace and light will do more than you can imagine for everyone involved; negative ego emotion will only lead to more suffering and separation.

Tom Carpenter says in *Healing the Dream* CD, "Be willing to be that light. Sit in chaos and turmoil and say there is an alternative" (Carpenter and Carpenter 2007). This won't be easy. It's easier to get sucked back in by the ego mind-set that will be churning up all around you in a million different conversations. *This is not about spouting off your newfound belief system at inappropriate times; it's about holding the truth in your mind.* If an opportunity arises in which you do feel guided to share that different perception, then please do—but it should never be forced. If you feel that you have to *prove* what you believe, you will find yourself under the ego's control once again, where *being right* is more important than *being peaceful.*

If you feel that you have to *prove* what you believe, you will find yourself under the ego's control once again, where *being right* is more important than *being peaceful.*

Sometimes people are ready to hear an alternative; always ask for guidance from Holy Spirit, your higher self, before you say a word. Remember, don't judge them for their ego, but find compassion in your heart as you empower them by holding the truth in your mind for them and yourself.

Dropping Others' Walls

My husband, Mark, is one of those rare people who naturally goes through life in a pretty present state of mind. He has a natural gift to help other people drop their walls. Mark will strike up a conversation anywhere with anybody. In the beginning of our relationship, it caused some distress for me. I realized my distress came from not wanting to bother people or take up too much of their time (again, a side-effect of my shyness and insecurity). It took me awhile to get over my own resistance to how Mark communicated with *everyone.*

When I was able to let go of some of my own fear and insecurity in regard to this, I realized that my husband has a gift. Mark can start a conversation with a total stranger who has the sourest expression on their face and the biggest ego wall surrounding them. Whereas I wouldn't want to bother this person, Mark sees straight through their ego wall and smiles and talks to them. I watch in amazement as they look up, make eye contact with him, and know (usually subconsciously) that he sees through their defensive wall. Mark sees them for who they really are, which melts their ego wall automatically. Suddenly that person has a smile on their face! They are sharing or responding to whatever he just said. He is engaging and connecting with someone who probably needed it the most.

I'll never forget the first phone message Mark left on my voicemail when he was calling me to ask me out. I replayed the message over and over again. This was the first time I had ever heard his voice, and you know what I thought? *I don't hear any ego in this guy's voice.* I was so used to being able to pick up that sound of insecurity covered up by that ego wall, but Mark didn't have that. He does have an ego that comes out from time to time, but it is very minimal and he is very aware of it.

I have learned more from this man than from any book that I have ever read in terms of really being present with people and his gift to drop people's walls automatically. Now I realize our child has this gift also. Our daughter is four and a half right now. She has no walls up yet. She is totally open and loving with most people she meets and the affect on them is miraculous to watch.

Whenever we go through a drive-thru, Rowen wants to know the name of the person taking our order. This used to stress me out because I never wanted to bother the busy person working at the window. But Rowen is persistent and she would push me until I eventually would ask the person in the window, "So, what's your name?" and they would look at me like I was crazy and about to ask them out on a date. I would begin to ramble, "Well, my little girl is in the back seat, and she has to know everybody's name..."

All of a sudden, these people at the window were looking in the back seat and smiling at my little girl. They were telling her their name, and she was responding back like any four-year-old child would. "Ooh, that's a silly name!" or "That's a pretty name!" Then, we were all laughing, connecting, and having this moment of being present and real with each other.

This has happened many times, and it still happens. One day, when we were driving away from a drive-thru window, I asked Rowen why she wanted to know everybody's name. She answered, "So that when I get bigger, I can talk to them." I broke into tears at the simple innocence and godliness of her actions. Why shouldn't we take more time to interact with people, even if it's a simple moment? Why shouldn't we take the time to ask someone their name, look them in the eye, and have that moment of connection? I realize what a gift it is to have these two in my life, always reminding me that there aren't really any walls except the imaginary ones we build. What once seemed like an impenetrable ego wall can be torn down instantaneously with a simple smile and an acknowledgment.

> What once seemed like an impenetrable ego wall can be torn down instantaneously with a simple smile and an acknowledgment.

Like ACIM says, *every* encounter can be a holy encounter. Every day presents a chance for you to see past the ego and be a truth-holder for your brother and the world. Give this gift of truth-holding to yourself and *everyone* you come into contact with.

> Every day presents a chance for you to see past the ego and be a truth-holder for your brother and the world.

In the next chapter, we will discuss what makes this whole process of awakening worth it—a life of absolute spiritual fulfillment and the subsequent, effortless ability to change our world for the better— otherwise known as an exquisite life!

CHAPTER 23

Absolute Spiritual Fulfillment & Step 6 to Awakening

When his mind, intellect, and self are under control, freed from restless desire, so that they rest in the spirit within, a man becomes a Yukta—one in communion with God.
—Krishna speaking to Arjuna in the *Bhagavad Gita* as referenced in B.K.S. Iyengar's book, *Light on Yoga* (Iyengar 1979, 19)

So What Is Absolute Spiritual Fulfillment?

Absolute spiritual fulfillment is what life is like when you live *awake:*

You will be guided through life effortlessly.
You will tap into unlimited creativity and connection as Spirit as you are *inspired.*
You will live in harmony with Creation.
You will bring more peace and positive change into your life, the lives around you, and the world around you as well.

Now, you are no longer experiencing spiritual starvation in which you are completely immersed in ego consciousness constantly looking for things outside of yourself to fill you up with no seeming way out. Now you have shifted more from ego consciousness to witness consciousness so that you can stay connected with your higher self and remember the bigger picture throughout anything that comes up. Now each time you shift from consciousness to pure awareness you bring more of that perfection from that higher state of awareness back into consciousness.

That's how transformational these altered states really are, and why it is so important for us to make living awake a priority.

Once you begin living awake it doesn't mean life is always perfect. You may have moments in which you find yourself immersed again in that ego cloud and that's okay. Living awake means that even when you find yourself back in that ego cloud, you now have an idea of what's going on and how to go about poking your head back out again. The ego can no longer make you feel as if it has completely blocked out the light. Allelujah!

Spiritual Fulfillment: What It *Doesn't* Look Like

You won't be running around with a crazy smile plastered on your face all the time. Look at people like Deepak Chopra and Eckhart Tolle; they have a serene countenance, reflecting the peace and joy inside.

When a person is overly excited and running around telling you how happy he is, there is a sense of false happiness. It is an ego emotional high just waiting to be stopped in its tracks for the emotional low that's on its way. When you see others in this emotional state, don't get caught up in the ego trap of judging them. Ask Holy Spirit to help you both remember your true nature in Spirit as perfect, whole, and eternal. There may be excitement or even passion, but it's from the joy of sharing this light with others, not from trying to convince others of your happiness and joy.

You can also recognize when people get caught up in being a little too serious with their spiritual path. Again, it doesn't mean you won't be completely serious about your path, but not in any exclusive or competitive kind of way. Work to understand the true difference between intentions coming from ego and intentions coming from Spirit. When intentions are coming from ego, there is a sense of inequality: "I'm happier than you are" or "I'm more serious

> When intentions are coming from ego, there is a sense of inequality: "I'm happier than you are" or "I'm more serious than you are." When these intentions are coming from Spirit, there is a sense of inclusion as you want to share your happiness and joy with others which is true fulfillment.

than you are." When these intentions are coming from Spirit, there is a sense of inclusion as you want to share your happiness and joy with others which is true fulfillment. But even more so, there is the realization that everyone else already has as much peace, joy, wholeness, and perfection as you do—they may just not realize it yet.

Be Guided through Life Effortlessly

When you have strengthened your connection to and trust in Holy Spirit, you will be tuned in to your inner guidance, your intuition. You will be guided by this intuition and guided through life effortlessly. You will no longer be driven through life by the analytical, thinking ego mind.

If you are still having trouble with this one, continue with the yoga practices. The practices will lead you to a state of being present in which you have unlimited access to guidance.

If there is something specific you need help with or an answer for, set the following intention for your practice: "Holy Spirit, help me be open to your guidance. Through my intuition, show me the answers I seek." Then allow a particular situation you need guidance about to come to mind. Forget all about your situation for the rest of the practice as you get present, get quiet, and allow witness consciousness to help you to release any stored stress.

At the end of the practice, when you are completely empty and quiet, notice if there is an answer for you in the form of an overwhelming feeling of what to do or what not to do with this particular situation. If there's not a clear-cut answer, it may be too early for you to make a choice or a final decision. Don't fret about it; the answer will come when you are ready.

Tap into Unlimited Creativity and Connection as Spirit

When you release big chunks of the ego through yoga practice, daily life situations, and relationship interactions, you clear the cloud of ego to reveal your true nature. Your true nature in Spirit is perfect, whole, and eternal, and you feel deeply your connection with all of creation.

From here, you have all the possibilities of creation at your fingertips and all for the good of the whole. No more feelings of worthlessness or inadequacy as the ego blocks you from your creative center.

Every moment in life is an opportunity for us to create and connect. It may be as simple as making a Halloween costume for our child, a handmade note for a friend, or as complex as some creative way to bring people together in your community. When we are present and connected, we will be filled with many opportunities to express our creativity and connection with others.

Live in Harmony with All of Creation

Find peace in every relationship. Find peace in every encounter. Find peace with all of your decisions. Find peace even amid the turmoil. You will no longer experience uncomfortable ego resistance or judgment.

Remember, if you can allow each experience in life to be experienced fully, with no resistance, it will always lead back to peace. So with anything negative that comes your way, stay present, allow yourself to experience it fully, and don't resist. Don't cling. Don't judge. Allow the peace to wash over you as if nothing ever happened. If ego takes over, it's okay. Forgive and accept and be at peace anyway.

If you are not at peace and not living in harmony with creation, then you are probably clinging to (*raga*) or resisting (*dvesha*) a particular situation or emotion and not letting it go. Allow yourself to get back into the self-study, figure out what you are clinging to (or resisting), and move through the practice of connecting with Holy Spirit and allowing the practice to do what it does best.

More Peace and Positive Change

The most important thing for any of us to be doing is to practice yoga as seated or movement meditation or really *anything* that brings us into this higher state of pure awareness. When we come back into consciousness we bring guidance as to how we can live more peaceful, loving lives. We come back into consciousness with the desire to extend this peace and love to everyone around us. We draw back from this Spiritual realm (what quantum physicists refer to as the realm of infinite possibilities) new creative solutions to before seen "problems". We draw back infinite guidance as to how we can live our lives in the best way possible for ourselves, our loved ones, and the world around us. The more we let go into this higher state of awareness, the more perfection from this spiritual realm we draw back into our consciousness. It doesn't have to be long periods of time spent in meditation. It can be short, simple moments of letting go of the thinking mind and allowing yourself to drop into pure awareness.

Dr. Goswami says:

> We practice. If some of us could *be good, do good*; practice *do, be, do* regularly; *be* with God some of the time, *be* in ego some of the time; and let the dance generate creative acts of transformation, that if we do just a certain threshold, I think very quickly we can achieve the power of downward position in unprecedented numbers. The threshold that will carry us towards making that fundamental step that these changes will take hold in all of humanity, just not in a few of us, but the few of us will start this. I invite you to be a quantum activist with this resolution, with this objective in mind: we can change ourselves and we can change the world simultaneously. (Goswami 2009)

If each one of us made it our priority to live life awake just think what the world would look like. And what Dr. Goswami is saying is that it doesn't even take all of us doing this to make big positive shifts in humanity and the world in which we live. It only takes a few. What better incentive to choose Spirit now and live a life awake?!

Step 6 to Awakening: Awaken Beyond Self, Beyond Ego, Beyond Choice, into Your True Nature as Pure Awareness

We really have to go beyond all self (even the true self) in order to shift into the experience of our true nature. This might seem scary at first, but as I've mentioned before, there is nothing scary about it. Remember, awakening is called "the cosmic joke" because it really is so simple. You've already had many moments of full awakening without realizing!

It's as simple as shifting out of the made-up ego mental construct, into witness consciousness, and finally into what yoga calls pure awareness. Now we are *in* the experience of life again, just like when we were babies. We are no longer experiencers of life, because we have let go of the self completely. We have no more thoughts, beliefs, judgments, or resistances to the experience of life. From here, we are *in* the experience of spiritual perfection, wholeness, and the knowledge of our eternal nature.

Welcome to your true nature.

We can rest in our true nature as pure awareness for a short moment or for eternity. The point is, we are always *in* this state of pure awareness, we just have to let all of the other "stuff" (ego consciousness and even witness consciousness) go enough to sink into the experience of this pure awareness. Sutra 25 in Chapter 4 of the *Yoga Sutras* says, "As soon as one can distinguish between consciousness and awareness, the ongoing construction of the self ceases." (Cope 2006, 292) By familiarizing ourselves more and more with these steps to awakening we increase our ability to distinguish between consciousness and awareness and we no longer continue to build this false mental construct of the ego. As we strengthen our relationship with and trust in our higher self, we live from witness consciousness (unbounded consciousness) and pure awareness more often, no longer ignorantly and maddeningly immersed in the ego. Now we are living life awake.

Don't let the ego take hold and convince you that living a life fully awake is impossible. This is exactly why more of us are not experiencing it, because the ego convinces us that we are unworthy, inadequate, and too darn bad. If God created us in *His* image, which He did, then we *are* worthy, we *are* adequate, and we are *not only* inherently good—we are inherently *perfect*.

convinces us that we are unworthy, inadequate, and too darn bad. If God created us in *His* image, which He did, then we *are* worthy, we *are* adequate, and we are *not only* inherently good—we are inherently *perfect.*

When in Doubt, Practice

The practices are meant to automatically bring you into the experience of your true nature in Spirit, into the experience of pure awareness as whole, perfect, and eternal. When in doubt of anything, go back to the practice. The practice gives you the experience of *awakening.* Don't underestimate it.

When you bring this awareness of your true nature as whole, perfect, and eternal back into your consciousness, there is *nothing* you or anyone else can do to disturb your peace of mind. Let's say that one again: *When you bring this awareness of your true nature as whole, perfect, and eternal back into your consciousness, there is nothing you or anyone else can do to disturb your peace of mind.*

Welcome to an exquisite life.

Awakened at Last

I'm going to leave you with my most favorite quote, a passage from the Bhagavad Gita, an ancient Indian poem in which Krishna, who is God, is speaking to a man named Arjuna. This particular quote came from an excerpt of the Bhagavad Gita quoted in B.K.S. Iyengar's book *Light on Yoga.*

> When his mind, intellect and self are under control, freed from restless desire, so that they rest in the spirit within, a man becomes a Yukta—one in communion with God. A lamp does not flicker in a place where no winds blow; so it is with a yogi, who controls his mind, intellect and self, being absorbed in the spirit within him. When the restlessness of the mind, intellect and self is stilled through the practice of Yoga, the yogi by the grace of the Spirit within himself finds fulfillment. Then he knows the joy eternal which is beyond the pale of the senses which

his reason cannot grasp. He abides in this reality and moves not therefrom. He has found the treasure above all others. There is nothing higher than this. He who has achieved it, shall not be moved by the greatest sorrow. This is the real meaning of Yoga—a deliverance from contact with pain and sorrow.

—Krishna speaking to Arjuna in the Bhagavad
Gita as referenced in B.K.S. Iyengar's book
Light on Yoga (Iyengar 1979, 19)

My Family

After a CT scan revealed a blood clot in my mom's aorta and a tumor in her lung, my family banded together around her, just like we did when we were kids during the nightly dramas. My mom's boyfriend barely left her side in the hospital that week. My brother, sister, and I were back and forth from work and taking care of kids to the hospital. My dad visited and, being a retired neurologist, kept up with what the doctors were telling us through conversations with my brother, an ophthalmologist.

The lung cancer was initially thought to be a rapid-growth cancer for which she would need to start chemo immediately or it could take her in weeks. We were all taken aback at the thought of the loss of our mother. She is the typical Southern Momma, the center point of our family, drawing us all into her house for holidays and birthdays and her excellent home cooking. We had noticed she was getting more tired over the past year, but none of us expected this—even though she was a heavy smoker.

I made sure I told my mom that I loved her and that I knew she loved us and had great, loving relationships with all of us. I let her know how much I would miss her if it was her time, but I knew I would always be able to talk with her and communicate with her. Mom told us that she wasn't afraid of dying because she had friends and family already over there. She just thought she would have more time with us, her children and grandchildren.

Three days later, we found out the good news. This lung cancer was not the rapid growth they thought but a different slow-growing cancer

213

called neuro-endocrine carcinoid, which could easily be cut out if there was not cancer in other areas. A clear bone scan and abdominal scan showed there was no other cancer.

Now we are waiting on her clot to clear enough for surgery. My mom's boyfriend, David, and my siblings and I went to her oncologist appointment with her two days ago. My dad was kept in the loop by phone. It's amazing to watch my siblings band together around Mom just like we did as kids. My brother, Curtis, the peacekeeper, now the doctor and protective first son, is making sure everything is made clear for us and that Mom has the utmost care from the most intelligent and talented doctors. Underneath this automatic role playing out, I notice the look of a surprised little boy who might lose his mother and a determination that he won't waste another minute on harboring resentment for the past. My sister, Suzette, the rebel, now a mother of three girls of her own, is making sure there is an organized and clear cut plan laid out for Mom's treatment (and making damn sure that my mother understands that she is quitting smoking *for good* this time). Underneath this automatic role playing out, I notice the look of a little girl clinging on to her mother's skirts, wide-eyed and fearful at the possibility of losing the center point of her compass. My Mom, our rock and our world, is now being so peaceful and brave.

David, Mom's boyfriend who's known her since they were kids, is loving and supporting my Mom plain and simple. I notice him trying to hide the fear and grief that is written all over his face, to no avail. My husband, Mark, my sister-in-law, Paige, and brother-in-law, Juan, are each doing all they can to support us by surrounding us all with strength, energy, and love. My dad is concerned, compassionate, supportive, and caring. I now realize that even though he and Mom are no longer married, they enjoy a forever friendship—a friendship built on the love they share for their kids, the love they share of the good memories, and the love they share for each other as fellow souls choosing to live this life together as friends, spouses, and then friends again.

And then there's me, Ginger, the observer, taking it all in and experiencing the gratitude for having these lovely beings as my family members here in this lifetime. Realizing that all the hurts that had been a part of our family's past were nothing more than forgiveness opportunities for us each to awaken more fully to the eternal connection between us all. Here in this moment of facing our mom's possible death, the past is forgiven, the past is forgotten, and the past is healed. We all are healed. My family is healed. I am grateful that my parents, my siblings, and I are in places in our lives in which forgiveness and love can come so easily.

When faced with the possible death of my mother, my belief that there is so much more than just this fleeting lifetime—that can be over in the blink of an eye—really hit home for me. I know that when I do have to face the deaths of others close to me, I will know without a doubt that nothing can truly take them from me. We are as God created us: whole, perfect, and eternal. We are One, we are One, we are One. I am infinitely grateful to share this experience with my family for however long it will last, while knowing the truth of our Oneness, our eternal connection in Spirit. I love you all.

Mom's Take on This Book

I asked my mom to read this before I sent it off to a publisher. She called me after reading the first half and said, "Ginger, I've done this. I know what you are talking about." She read me *A Prayer to the Holy Spirit* by Cardinal Mercier that she had read every night when she was going through her divorce. She said it got her through. She said that what I had written about in this book was what she felt she had been doing over the last several years, "in her own, Catholic kind of way," but she knew what I was explaining from a yogic and a Course standpoint to be true.

As she was telling me this, I realized how quickly the walls are falling down around us that seem to separate us. Things are changing. We are collectively moving toward seeing this union, this connection with each other. We are moving

> I realized how quickly the walls are falling down around us that seem to separate us. Things are changing. We are collectively moving toward seeing this union, this connection with each other. We are moving toward becoming a more loving, forgiving people as Jesus teaches us to be.

toward becoming a more loving, forgiving people as Jesus teaches us to be.

ChooseSpiritNow.com

Remember, if you want to experience this book as an *online retreat*, check out *ChooseSpiritNow.com*. CSN Retreat acts as a supplement to this book and is one more reminder tool to help keep you in your awakening, bringing more peace and positive change into your life, the lives around you, and the world around you as well. There are video presentations (which are the content and stories from this book in keynote form) and journaling exercises to keep you in your self-study. There are contemplative practices to help you go beyond the body, beyond the mind and into an experience of your true nature as Spirit. Enjoy!

Let's Do This Together

This is the gentle awakening, right here and right now. God has his hand on us and is gently rocking us, asking us to wake up and open our eyes to see clearly. Let's do this together. Let's help each other to overcome this dark cloud of ego mind and live in the light, peace, joy, and love of Spirit. We *can* do it. God Himself is our biggest ally. What have we to lose but the pain and suffering, isolation, and loneliness that seems to come from simply being human and having an ego-self? We have to look upon one another without judgment and with love and forgiveness. It is in doing this that we truly see God, truly experience His presence, truly make that choice between ego and Spirit, and cross that bridge between darkness and enlightenment. Once you make the choice for Spirit, it gets easier and easier. We have to put ourselves in the best position to choose Spirit now and find the love to forgive ourselves completely if we don't.

> We have to put ourselves in the best position to choose Spirit now and find the love to forgive ourselves completely if we don't.

Awakening is not some golden trophy
awaiting us after a long and arduous journey.
It is here for us, right here, right now.
It's in the details of how we live each moment

216

and the choices that we make.
Eventually we find ourselves beyond choice, beyond thought,
beyond the practices and in the awakening.
In the meantime, Choose Spirit Now.
My deepest gratitude in sharing this with you.
Namaste, the light in me is the light in you.
We are all One.
Namaste.

Conclusion

Choose Spirit Now teaches us that we have a choice and teaches us how to get to a place (witness consciousness) where we can make that choice: a choice to have our mind controlled by the ego or guided by Spirit, a choice to live in fear or live in love, a choice to believe we are humans who will die one day or eternal Spirit with no end, a choice for darkness or light, a choice to believe we are unequal or equal as One in Spirit, a choice to live in the illusion or the happy dream, a choice to be limited or limitless, a choice to live in dissatisfaction or to live in absolute Spiritual fulfillment—bringing forth positive change into the world and leading exquisite lives.

Will you choose to hold on to beliefs that bring fear, insecurity, guilt, and misery into your life? Or will you choose beliefs that bring love, joy, and peace into your life? *Are you ready to take responsibility for the life you want to live?* Are you ready to *choose Spirit now?*

RESOURCE LIST

Books

Adyashanti. 2011. *Falling into Grace.* Boulder: Sounds True Incorporated.

Brown, Sylvia and Lindsay Harrison. 2001. *Life on the Other Side.* New York: New American Library.

Cope, Stephen. 1999. *Yoga and the Quest for the True Self.* New York: Bantam Books.

_____. 2006. *The Wisdom of Yoga.* New York: Bantam Dell.

Forrest, Ana T. 2011. *Fierce Medicine.* New York: Harper Collins Publishers.

Foundation for *A Course in Miracles. 1992. A Course in Miracles,* Combined Volume Second Edition. Mill Valley: Foundation for Inner Peace.
(A Course in Miracles and ACIM are registered service marks and trademarks of the Foundation for A Course in Miracles.)

Hartranft, Chip. trans. 2003. "The Yoga Sutra in English." in Appendix B of *The Wisdom of Yoga,* by Stephen Cope. New York: Bantam Dell.

Iyengar, B.K.S. 1979. *Light on Yoga.* New York: Schocken Books.

Levitt, Atma Jo Ann. comp. editor. 2004. *Pilgrim of Love: The Life and Teachings of Swami Kripalu.* New York: Monkfish Book Publishing Company.

Mascaro, Juan. trans. 2003. *The Bhagavad Gita*. Brodbeck, Simon, Introduction. London: Penguin Books.

McCourt, Frank. 1999. *Angela's Ashes*. New York: Touchstone.

Mitchell, Stephen. trans. and intro. 2000. *Bhagavad Gita: A New Translation*. New York: Three Rivers Press.

Northrup, Christiane MD. 2002. *Women's Bodies Women's Wisdom*. New York:Bantam Books.

Renard, Gary R. 2004. *The Disappearance of the Universe*. Carlsbad: Hay House, Inc.

Roberts, Bernadette. 1991. *The Path to No-Self: Life at the Center*. Albany: State University of New York Press.

Shearer, Alistair. trans. and intro. 1982. *The Yoga Sutras of Patanjali*. New York: Bell Tower.

Veiera, Tomas, and Nouk Sanchez. 2007. *Take Me to Truth: Undoing the Ego*. Washington DC: O Books.

Williamson, Marianne. 1992. *Return to Love: Reflections on the Principles of A Course in Miracles*. New York: Harper Collins Publishers.

CDs/DVDs

Carpenter, Tom and Linda Carpenter. 2007. *Healing the Dream* CD. Princeville: tlcx2@earthlink.net.

Carpenter, Tom, and Robert Holden, PhD. 2010. *A Dialogue on Forgiveness* DVD. London: Owl Productions.

Cope, Stephen. 2004. *Four Functions of the Transformation Teacher* CD. Pittsfield: Kripalu Yoga Teachers Association.

Faulds, Danna. 2011. *Poems from the Heart of Yoga* CD. Pittsfield: Kripalu Yoga Teachers Association.

Goswami, Amit PhD. 2009. *Quantum Activist* DVD. Yachats: Bluedot Productions.

Hartman, Devarshi Stephen. 2013. *The Essence of the Bhagavad-Gita* CD. Pittsfield: Kripalu Yoga Teachers Association.

Veiera, Tomas and Nouk Sanchez. 2009. *The Miracle of Trust: Overcoming the One Obstacle to Love's Infinite Presence* Audio CD. Boulder: Sounds True, Incorporated.

Websites

Martin Luther King, Jr.. BrainyQuote.com, Xplore Inc, 2014. http://www.brainyquote.com/quotes/quotes/m/martinluth103425.html, accessed July 26, 2014.

Emoto, Masaru. 2010. Accessed July 25, 2014. *http://www.masaru-emoto.net/english/water-crystal.html*.

Wikipedia, 2014. "Brihadaranyaka Upanishad 1.3.28." last modified April 15. *http://en.wikipedia.org/wikiBrihadaranyaka_Upanishad*.

CPSIA information can be obtained at www.ICGtesting.com
Printed in the USA
LVOW11s0021130215

426829LV00002B/75/P

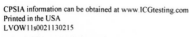

9 781452 598277